THIS AND THAT

Emily Carr, **B.C. Forest**, c. 1938-39, oil on paper,
Art Gallery of Greater Victoria, 34 x 22 in,
AGGV, 1984.050.002, Ruth Humphrey Estate

This and That

The Lost Stories of Emily Carr

edited by Ann-Lee Switzer

Victoria • Vancouver • Calgary

TouchWood Editions
#108 – 17665 66A Avenue
Surrey, BC V3S 2A7
www.touchwoodedition.com

TouchWood Editions
PO Box 468
Custer, WA
98240-0468

Library and Archives Canada Cataloguing in Publication
Carr, Emily, 1871–1945.
This and that: the lost stories of Emily Carr / edited by Ann-Lee Switzer.

ISBN 978-1-894898-61-4

1. Carr, Emily, 1871–1945—Anecdotes. 2. Painters—British Columbia—Anecdotes. 3. Carr, Emily, 1871–1945—Family. 4. Carr, Emily, 1871–1945. 5. Painters—British Columbia—Biography. I. Switzer, Ann-Lee II. Title.

ND249.C3A2 2007b   759.11   C2007-902357-6

Library of Congress Control Number: 2007926468

Interior design by G. R. Switzer
Cover painting by Emily Carr, B.C. Forest (detail), c. 1938-39, oil on paper, Art Gallery of Greater Victoria

Printed in Canada

TouchWood Editions acknowledges the financial support for its publishing program from the Government of Canada through the Book Publishing Industry Development Program (BPIDP), Canada Council for the Arts, and the province of British Columbia through the British Columbia Arts Council and the Book Publishing Tax Credit.

BRITISH COLUMBIA ARTS COUNCIL
Supported by the Province of British Columbia

Canada Council for the Arts   Conseil des Arts du Canada

This book has been produced on 100% post-consumer recycled paper, processed chlorine free and printed with vegetable-based dyes.

To Ira my friend and to a little far away
girl to whom he chose to give the name of "Small"

CONTENTS

AUTHOR'S NOTE

What are Hundreds and Thousands? Why should I call my book by that name?

Hundreds and Thousands are an English kind of candies, so tiny that they have neither flavour, crunch, nor colour, each in her own right. One single candy would only fill a cavity in your tooth, but when spilled in quantity over a Christmas or birthday-cake, they make it a glory, sprinkled over the snow white icing. They were blue, pink, red and yellow and they make a delicious crunch. A deliciousness compounded of hundreds of nothings.

Father kept a great jar of Hundreds and Thousands on the sample shelf in his office. After an attack of gout, Mother sometimes sent the three little girls, Bigger, Middle and Small, down to his office with a hot lunch of soup in a small stone jar (the thermos bottle was then unknown). The jar was rolled in many newspapers and wrapped in a white napkin and set in a little basket. We sat on the visitor chairs while Father ate. When the napkin was folded and put back in the little basket with the jar, then Father said, "Hold out your hands," and out came three pair of palms up. One pair was spotless, one nearly clean and one pair grubby. Down bobbed three heads as Father poured and then out came three tongues, crunch, crunch, crunch.

A plain brown cake is good enough but an iced cake with Hundreds and Thousands over her snow is something beyond good enough. The gay little nothings, the Hundreds and Thousands, have transformed it. It is the same in life, even a life which we thought has been drab while we were living it; if you look back and pick out the little events nearly forgotten, you find, that each has touched you or teased you or did something funny which had helped to make life interesting, crunchy, sweet, delicious.

There is no sequence to my Hundreds and Thousands. I have just picked up a few little happenings here and there. Some of the littlest taught me the most, some of the apparent biggest were really insignificant.

I have chosen to call this collection of tiny stories, things that happened any time through my life, Hundreds and Thousands, because they are too small each to be taken singly. But each, complete in itself, serves to ornament life which would be a drab affair without the little things we do not even notice or think of at the time but which old age memory magnifies.*

Emily Carr

* *Emily wrote two slightly different versions of an Introduction for the work she intended to call "Hundreds and Thousands." One version is printed in full above. This last paragraph is the final paragraph of the second version of her Introduction.*

EDITOR'S INTRODUCTION

On October 4, 1943, while recovering from a stroke, the Canadian artist Emily Carr (1871–1945) wrote to her editor and friend Ira Dilworth from the Royal Jubilee Hospital in Victoria, British Columbia:

> You will grin when I say I have made a few feeble scratchings towards *something else*. A few stray thoughts . . . [1]

Two days later she wrote:

> I brought in an old exercise book and a thought or two began to wiggle . . . My new write is a hodge-podge. It is at *present* called 'Hundreds and Thousands.' Did you have those tiny tiny colored candies you sprinkled over birthday cakes or rolled soft chocolates in 'til they coated like a barnacle? . . . These little jottings are *too small* to call stories. They are just little isolated incidences told as *clean cut & briefly* as I can. Each a separate little unit with a thought tied up in it. They will [be] here & there picked from my 70 years.[2]

Sick as she was, Emily Carr was on a roll towards "something else"—a new project conceived by her and carried out entirely on her own. She was still working on "Hundreds and Thousands" just before she died. Perhaps it was medicine for her. Her physician Dr. Baillie was a fan of her writing and encouraged her to continue doing it, in moderation.

Over the next year and a half, she developed the original "50 little stories or incidents...roughly suggested"[3] that she had jotted down when in the hospital, into almost-finished stories. On February 14, 1945, two weeks before she died, Emily wrote to Ira:

> I am glad you enjoyed Hundreds and Thousands. I've written two since. I am *not* surprised that many need rewriting. Next batch will be small only 10-15. I found so many confusing. You are not to press yourself to crit but just read for fun at present ... many of the others I sent you were too long, not concise enough. I must try and just pick out the core of the thought and wean the extra round it ... Suddenly with the talking, a hundred characters will pop into my head but I must [write] or it eludes me. I write down on any scrap of paper ... [4]

During her lifetime, Emily Carr saw three collections of her stories published: *Klee Wyck* (1941), *The Book of Small* (1942), and *The House of All Sorts* (1944). At her request, her biography *Growing Pains* (1946) appeared posthumously. When she died, two more books were on their way and were eventually published as *The Heart of a Peacock* (1953) and *Pause: A Sketchbook* (1953). The actual realization of the works had been very much a collaborative effort among Ira Dilworth, the publisher William H. Clarke and Emily Carr. The order, titles and makeup of the books evolved over the last five years of Emily's life, with Ira continuing after her death.

Beginning with the publication of *Klee Wyck* in 1941, Emily Carr's reputation as a writer was quickly established, eclipsing her major vocation of painting in popularity. Her writing was able to touch people, a ray of sunshine during the dark years of World War II. It also spoke to the still-nascent Canadian national identity. *Klee Wyck* received a Canadian Governor General's Award for Literature published in 1941. During the next year, her audience widened beyond Canada, with the publication of *Klee Wyck* in Britain and the U.S.A.

Where did the writing voice of this highly-trained visual artist come from? In her writings, she confesses to feeling in her youth a need for written expression of the deep-seated thoughts she was unable to share with her family. (see "Topsy Tiddles" p. 4) Later, at various times, she recorded in journals the experiences of her travels and excursions. She kept up a voluminous correspondence with friends and family.

The love of language was instilled early; the reading of poetry, works of Dickens and other authors—and of course the Bible—was part of life at home. She loved poetry, committing poems to memory, and penned doggerel verse, often accompanied by humourous sketches. The love of poetry helped bond Carr and Dilworth; in many of the letters they exchanged, both quote favourite verses. In "The Round World" (p. 163) she reads Walt Whitman aloud to two German young men in the wilderness of the Malahat, outside Victoria.

Emily Carr did not do things by halves. She felt she needed more guidance than she was able to muster from her incomplete high school education. In October 1926 she signed up for a correspondence course in writing with the Palmer Institute of Authorship in Hollywood, California. The Institute sent her instruction books (preserved, complete with underlinings, in the British Columbia Archives) and she sent back her stories, which were read and returned with notes from the instructors. In 1934 she enrolled in courses at The Provincial Normal School (Victoria College). Her teacher at the College, Nellie de Bertrand Lugrin, later reminisced:

> She was original in her themes and treatment, but her grammatical construction was deplorable; and she admitted that there was not a worse speller in the world. Even at that when her work was corrected, it was chosen as the best in the class.[5]

The first-prize story was one of her Indian tales, "The Hully-Up Paper," which later appeared in *The Heart of a Peacock.*

Carr also shared her writing with some of her writing friends. Her "listening ladies," Flora Burns, Ruth Humphrey and Margaret Clay, all played a role in steering Carr's development. Independent-minded as she was, she often bristled at criticism:

> Once I wrote a story, and I gave it to seven of my friends to read. Every one of the seven returned the manuscript with a different complaint. If only they had even two of them found the same faults I would have been encouraged. Some of the crits went to my soul and touched it, some made the soles of my boots tickle to kick them.[6]

The most significant influence on Emily Carr's writing career was without a doubt Ira Dilworth (1894-1962), introduced to her by Ruth Humphrey. Former teacher at Victoria High School in his home town, later professor of English at the University of British Columbia, Dilworth was at the time of their first meeting director of the Vancouver branch of the Canadian Broadcasting Corporation. They began collaborating in 1939. Much has been written about the close relationship between Carr and Dilworth, and recently some of their correspondence has been published. A spiritual bond grew between the two, and Emily Carr came to trust and rely on him. They shared a love of poetry, written expression and the Canadian West. She trusted him, too, with her unfinished literary efforts, which were willed to him at her death. She had kept them in a locked steamer trunk, safe from prying eyes of visitors and helpers.

Ira Dilworth gave her confidence and guidance but was always respectful and tactful. For example, commenting on a group of animal stories which were eventually published in the *Heart of a Peacock,* he wrote Emily:

> The manuscript has been a great joy to me…as fine as anything
> in Small's book…I have made a number of suggestions which
> will help on the formal, mechanical side . . . (18 November 1942)[7]

Like her painting that expressed the world she saw in bold colours and few strokes, Emily Carr's style is concise and vivid. Her
biting wit pulls humour out of dark corners, and she shapes her
characters and surroundings with quick, sharp phrases.

> You know how ignorant I am when it comes to constructions
> & literary value. There are only two rules that I know in writ-
> ing[:] see the thing as *clear* as you can and try to *show* it never
> using *big* hard words where little ones will do. (18 January, 1942)[8]

She had an enormous persistence and patience when it came to
re-working her writing, just as she did with her artwork, the first
love of her life. In addition to "pruning" down to the core of meanings, and choosing "strong talk" over ordinary nouns and verbs,
inventing as needed for her expression, she was always:

> …diving into the attics & corners & feelings and half-seeing the
> reasons *why* for lots of things and plumbing deeper into things
> I'd skimmed… (21 December, 1942)[9]

Neither does she apologize for her unique approach:

> Mind you I'm going to write it in my own way. I'm going to use
> any person I like up [to] the tenth person plural if I've a mind
> to. If I can't get words that fit the occasion I'm going to make
> half-breed words from two that nearly fit. I'm going to use past
> present or future tense. All I care about in the whole book is just
> to get the thing across that I want to say.[10]

Her stories are compelling in their own right, simply because of
the unique situations she describes. But her use of language is also
key. She deliberately uses plain language and simple construction to

build her images and move the narrative. Yet her stories beg to be read aloud, as Ira Dilworth did on the radio even before the publication of *Klee Wyck*. At one point he even suggested to her that passages might be written in free-verse form.

Language for Carr was a means to an end; mechanics, grammar, or syntax were no obstacles. If no suitable word existed, she invented. Strong verbs abound. She often *boiled*. Auntie *hypocritted*. Sisters would *bridesmaid*. Her brother-in-law did not sing, he *vocalled* and *tremoloed*. Mr. Fell's corner was *sidwalked* especially fancy. She wanted to *blue-pill and black-draught* every member of the family. My personal favourite: Mrs. Fraser *onioned* lavishly. Then there are the Carr metaphors and similes. A suitcase was not just empty, it was *holding its own emptiness*. Mrs. Bales is compared to a *pear*, her husband to an *apple*. The corset saleswoman *might as well have been pushed into a drainpipe*. She gives her undesirables wicked verbal swipes: *The lunatic writhed cryings out of the violin; a falsely blond girl . . . violently lipsticked*. The full effect can be humourous, pathetic, poetic, or all those at once. Her style and her ways of "going deeper" are part of the reason she has had such a universal appeal. They are why Emily Carr has continued to grace our bookstore shelves these past sixty years.

Major biographies of Emily Carr have been published, by Edythe Hembroff-Schleicher (1978), Maria Tippett (1979) and Paula Blanchard (1988). Over the years, the literature about Emily Carr has grown, especially recently. Researchers were able to make use of Dilworth's papers which his nieces sold to the National Museum of Canada in 1967, which in turn presented them to the Provincial Archives of British Columbia. Among these treasures were the many stories she had written for her "Hundreds and Thousands" project, acknowledged in the biographers' notes as "unpublished stories." Her biographers realized of course that Carr was presenting herself as she wished to be remembered. She "storied" her life. She regularly made herself out to be much younger than she was and exaggerated the lack of success and acceptance of her art. This is not an unusual practice of autobiographers and should not surprise us. We also know that she deliberately set out to write stories, and used her experiences as a base for them. She found it difficult simply to invent characters and situations, just as she shunned pure abstraction in her painting. Through interviews of contemporaries and other documentation, we can round out the picture of this remarkable woman. It is hoped that these "new" stories will also add to our "hoard" of knowledge about her life and times.

The last major collection of Emily Carr's writing to be published, a selection from the journals that she kept from 1927 to 1941, came out in 1966. At first, the process of selecting and editing for publication was carried out by her publisher, William Clarke, and Ira Dilworth. In the midst of this labour, Ira died, in 1962. Ira Dilworth's nieces, Phylis Inglis and Edna Parnall, had inherited all their uncle's papers, including Carr's correspondence and the steamer trunk containing her manuscripts. Clarke carried on with the journals as best he could with some help from Phylis Inglis.

When the book appeared, it bore the title *Hundreds and Thousands*, a phrase taken from "a notebook found among Miss Carr's papers," according to its Preface (p. v). Ira Dilworth would have been the only one to know the true significance of the phrase. When the notebook passage turned up, likely an early draft of her Introduction to the present work, it seemed a good candidate for a title.

The confusion was compounded by the additional quotation, in the Publisher's Forward, of another passage from one of Emily's letters referring to "Hundreds and Thousands." "She even thought of the title," declares the Forward. We know now that she was referring to the stories of her last two years, not her journals.

For a long time I have been poking around in the original documents pertaining to the life of Emily Carr. I have spent many pleasant and astonishing hours, down the street from my apartment, in the B.C. Provincial Archives. Correspondence, diaries, photographs, taped interviews—there were so many facets, Emily Carr became a project and obsession. Why else would I choose an apartment in the sky with a view of both Carr House and House of All Sorts, two blocks away down below?

After perusing her unpublished manuscripts for awhile, I began to notice the phrase "Hundreds and Thousands" scribbled here and there at the tops of some of the unpublished stories. Clearly these had nothing to do with the published journals. A pattern seemed to emerge. Then I found not one but two Introductions to what appeared to be a collection of stories. And it was!

When the dust of discovery had settled, well over sixty stories had surfaced. Most were typed, probably by the author herself, with hand corrections, sometimes with several versions both handwritten and typed. Some were only handwritten drafts, on the backs of letters, on notebook paper and ledger-paper, even on the back of junk-mail solicitations. They varied in length from one to many pages. In addition to the two introductions, Carr had laid out two tables of contents which, though incomplete (and each in a different order), confirmed her intention to create a random collection of memories.

There was even a handwritten dedication to Ira and her childhood persona, Small, on a separate paper (the dedication used in this volume) and another dedication at the bottom of the manuscript of "The Family Plot" (p. 80): "Ira from Small / From Hundreds & Thousands which is to be dedicated to Ira Dilworth / 1944." None of the stories had ever been published, although there are overlaps in subject matter with her published stories. Sometimes the most astonishing things are hidden before our very eyes.

Because she was working up to the "last minute," none of the "Hundreds and Thousand" stories reached final form, much less were they overseen by her "Eye" (Ira Dilworth). The unpublished stories were cuddled together with other writings in the trunk that she willed to Ira. I am not even sure if all are "Hundreds and Thousands," for she did not put them all in the Table of Contents, and not all of them have the designation at the top of the page. Some may very well be "oddments"—to use one of Emily's favoured words.

When going over the stories for print, I tried to adhere to the instructions she gave to Ira, her editor, which were to care for spelling, punctuation and other mechanics, but also to prune for shape. In some cases there are multiple versions that I have combined. Not every story has been included. Some were too long, or repeated themes already covered, or else they did not seem to fit her criteria. Ira Dilworth was respectful of retaining the voice of the author, and I hope I have been guided by that spirit.

Then there was the problem of the title. It had already been used, although not appropriately, for a published work. While re-reading Carr's writings, I was on the lookout for some other phrase to use for this book. "Oddments" does recur, but did not seem quite right. Then in "The Round World" (p. 166) a phrase jumped out.

Emily receives a Christmas package from her young German friend Gerhard containing mementos from his stay in Arizona: "They sent me a little box of small out-of-the-way bits of nothings, desert flowers pressed, twigs of *this and that*, and the warmest greetings." (italics added) "This and that"— bits of nothings ... like the little candies! The phrase resonated. How many of us do that, save a subway ticket, a woodpecker feather, a bent bottle cap? And even years later find them in the cupboard and can't bear to garbage them, because each opens a memory of a specific time and place? *This and That*, admittedly a poor second to what Emily had planned, will have to do for now. A scattering of happenings, snapshots, this and that, from a life lived to the full—that is what you are about to read.

The Real Hundreds and Thousands has stood up at last, Emily Carr's collection of snippets of memory, drawn from the whole of her life, to be sprinkled randomly like tiny candies on a cake, for all to savour. That this project was underway during the physical suffering of the last year and a half of her life is testament to Emily Carr's tenacious spirit and determination. It is 40 years exactly since the publication of Hundreds and Thousands—the Journals. It could be said that Hundreds and Thousands—The Stories had its birth at the Royal Jubilee Hospital in Victoria. I hope that Emily Carr and her child-self Small will give their indulgence to this effort and correction, this cake which has finally had its just desserts.

Ann-Lee Switzer
Victoria, B.C.
December 13, 2006

NOTES:

1. *Corresponding Influence: Selected Letters of Emily Carr and Ira Dilworth,* Ed. Linda M. Morra, Toronto: University of Toronto Press, 2006, p.234.

2. Ibid., p. 235.

3. Ibid., p. 239.

4. *Opposite Contraries, the Unknown Journals of Emily Carr and Other Writings,* Ed. Susan Crean, Vancouver: Douglas & McIntyre, 2003, p.240.

5. *Victoria Sunday Times,* September 22, 1951, p. 3.

6. From an unpublished manuscript in the British Columbia Archives and Records Service. (BCARS), Inglis Collection, MS 2181, box 9, folder 1.

7. Morra, p. 170-1.

8. Ibid., p. 100-1.

9. Ibid., p. 180.

10. Unpublished manuscript in the BCARS, see note 6 above.

This and That

or
the real

"Hundreds and Thousands"

HAPPY, HAPPY CHILDREN

The electric bulb over our bed was still swaying when I opened my eyes. It was evident someone had just switched it on. By the clock it was early morning. By the hole in the sky which was the open dormer window it was little beyond the murk of daybreak. I tore my eyes from sleep and sat up; Middle[1] was sitting up beside me blinking but calm. What churned the wonderment over and over in our eyes was the sight of a near and elderly neighbour seated on the foot of our bed, crying. She was saying over and over, "Happy, happy children! You have a Mother in Heaven."

The lady had apparently dressed in great haste. All her buttons seemed to have shot clear of the eye-holes. She had on a mouse colour canton flannel dressing-gown, half a dozen buttons squabbling for one buttonhole. Her iron grey hair was in a little plaited snarl and aggressively poked round the far cheek. One hand clutched a morsel of grey worsted shawl to her throat, while the other held a miscellany of garments, and prominently and unmistakably a white pair

1. Middle *was Emily Carr's sister* **Alice**, *two years older.* **Emily** *called her childhood self* Small. *Other siblings were:* **Elizabeth** *or* Bigger, *four years older than Emily;* **Clara** *or* Tallie, *14 years older;* **Edith** *or* the Elder, *15 years older; and the youngest and only boy of the family was* **Richard** *or* Dick *in her stories, four years younger. Emily was born in 1871, the year British Columbia joined Canada.*

of trimmed drawers too wide for sleeves. A little button-up top garment, darted and boned, hung over her wrist. Her hand was through the armhole. Several hairpins were in her mouth. As I looked she moved.

She ducked forward to administer a series of lip-noises. They began at Middle's forehead, and straggled up and down her cheek like wild geese migrating in a high sky, all of a flock but each goose separate. Her kisses were like that, and her skin smelled old and dry and furry. I was glad that, tucked in between Middle and the wall, I was out of kissing range.

Slowly the house was bringing back yesterday to me—but yesterday we had a mother in the room just steps away, up a few stairs on the next landing. Yesterday we had been kept from school and the house was quiet. Father was home all day and not a bit cross. He sat by Mother's bedside and held her hand. He could not enjoy his food or his garden or his grapevine. He could not even enjoy his temper. It had forsaken him with his appetite. Everyone was trying to behave as usual and could not.

When it came to saying good night Mother held us each in her weak arms. It was very late when we went to bed. Now this was the next day.

"What does she mean?" I said to Middle. "Is Mother dead?"

Middle said with a sob, "I suppose so."

But that was not enough for me. I climbed over the foot of the bed, not an easy feat. It was one of the old-fashioned spool kind and high. Now I started for the stairs. Middle and the old lady followed. Father was crossing the top landing. He did not speak. He went into his room and shut the door. Mother's door just opposite was open and the Elder was moving about inside. But the feel was quite different in the room. The old lady took each of us by a hand and led us to the bedside. There were no blankets on the bed, just a sheet and her night dress covered Mother, and she looked so thin and little. The Elder folded down the sheet from the face and Middle and I took a long long look. Mother not struggling to breathe! I was going to kiss her but the Elder snatched me back.

"It is not good," she said, "to kiss the dead."

Then Bigger came with a candle and said she would see the neighbour down to the front door and undo the bolt. That time Bigger was included in the "happy happy children" but Bigger was equal to her and gave her back chapters of texts. Then the old lady descended the stair, putting on clothing as she went. The Elder gathered a bundle of blankets to take downstairs to make up a bed for herself on the sofa. She had been sleeping in Mother's room.

"Do we have to go to bed again?"

"Yes."

Middle was always so quiet about things. She got in and was asleep before I had climbed over her.

"Middle, aren't grownups stupid?"

"Um, I s'pose so."

"Calling us 'happy children' over and over, when we never can be happy again and she knows it."

If she had said, "Unhappy me! I put both my feet in one drawer leg going downstairs and might have fallen and broken both legs," it would have been sensible talk and true. Crazy to step into those things going down steps!

TOPSY TIDDLES

Topsy Tiddles was not anybody. She was not wrought in flesh and blood, but existed as a boat exists in fog . . . there, but hidden. It came with fearful ardent rushing, this idea of Small's that she must say things, but she did not know how to. I don't mean just talk. "Everyone with a tongue can do that," Small told herself. "But I want to make my tongue and my heart work together." The tongue always gabbles away and leaves the heart stranded, because your heart is much shyer than your tongue.

Small had not read a great many books. The Elder often read Dickens aloud to the children in the evenings. Small loved that, and Small had a whole shelf of Poets over the top of her bed and she loved those, mulling dreamily over the poems as she went to sleep.

Small tried to write poetry; it appealed to her more than prose. Poetry took her into a new world when she read it, but she could not write it. She could just make silly jingles to go with caricatures that she drew of people. Just stupid things that tickled a laugh out of people. She wanted to write things different to that, things that played tunes on the expressions of people's faces, but she did not know how to begin.

That was not the worst of it either. Suppose people wrote of the puzzles and bewilderments, and suppose they got found, these worded puzzles and bewilderments and they were trodden on and laughed at—well it would hurt. Could one go on living for hurt? Small thought not. "So I'd die," concluded Small and went on getting more and more muddled.

Middle and she did not like the same things, no good discussing it with Middle. Neither did Bigger and brother Dick, who were four years too young and four years too old. I suppose all adolescent children grow too big to contain themselves in prose, so eventually in self-protection they have to expand in poetry. All young life is poetry, frightfully serious poetry. Words would help, but where does one find the right words, because think and say are not the same. There were always grown-ups to laugh!

Prose writers can say just the same things as poets, but it seems that except for good ones, their saying is not quite so right, as poetry meanings are apt to go silly. The prose writer kept within limits, wide expansive bounds maybe, but they had not the spring, the mystery of poetry. They had just as much or more truth. Prose was alright but poetry was more uplifting, at least that was the way it seemed to Small.

In the year her father gave Small *The Lady of the Lake*,[1] the Elder gave Bigger, Middle and Small each a diary, a big Letts[2] diary. The children were supposed to write in them every day. Bigger filled hers with religion, not her feelings towards it as much as a faithful record of goings to church, how much she put in the collection plate, a short resume of the sermon, the text and the names of the hymns.

1. *An epic poem by Sir Walter Scott, published in 1810.*

2. *From* Charles Letts of London, *a stationery firm founded in 1796, specialising in yearly diaries.*

Middle's diary was a chronicle of the births, deaths, and marriages of her doll family and her cats. Small's diary was almost empty except for repeated Monday entries: "Monday is our wash day," she wrote, "Mary comes to do it for Mother. Mary is an Indian."

It seemed to have been the great event of Small's life at that time, not so much the washing as the Indian. Here and there came an entry: "Father and I found a bird's nest in the hedge . . . The cow found a most lovely calf in the hay stack."

In looking through the diaries in after-years, Small's thought was this: All I wanted to say I dare not say more, nor did Bigger or Middle, because we felt that our diaries were supervised. We would have had much to say. Things about the world, about us, and to write about them would have taught us something and helped us to identify ourselves with nature. Our diaries were amusement for the elders.

Well, Small had not gained a thing from her diary as far as wording thoughts went. She was pretty young at the time of the diaries but when she became a big girl and was thinking harder, then the desire came again to express, so she invented the fictitious "Topsy."

"I'll give you a stupid name, so you won't even think you are real yourself, Topsy, and if I do, I'll remember you are not real and I won't be so shy of speaking straight to you. I'll write it in letters and I can think a think and come back to it again and add more thought to it because you've kept it there in my letter to you. I will write you a long, long letter."

There was one great drawback to Topsy which really was not her fault. Every place we had was still supervised for tidiness. I was not afraid of Middle reading Topsy. Though she and I shared all the space in our world that was ours, we did not quite share each other's thoughts. But Bigger and Elder snooped. They seemed to think that reading anything written by a younger sister was their duty—why you might even write a "love letter." Quite young girls did and it was disgraceful. The Elder and Bigger stamped with both feet on love, or supposedly so. Or you might write something about them! Young girls' correspondence certainly should be guided. It was the duty of our elders. They did it for your own sakes and sometimes they laughed and quoted your words back at you.

Small's first device was to change a good clear but perfectly characterless handwriting to an unintelligible scribble which even she herself could not read. Her next protective step was to climb to the most inaccessible places and hide the old exercise book which was arithmetic sums on one side and Topsy letters on the other.

Small had three chapters written. What with the long, long walk to and from school, the being kept in for arithmetic every day and the home work, there was not much time for Topsy. So Small got up a little earlier for her.

Ah, this lovely spring morning there was twenty minutes before she need leave for school! She dived into Topsy. Middle thought she was preparing her home work.

Bigger came rushing by the open door, shouted, "Girls! The clock is fifteen minutes slow, hurry, hurry!"

Middle seized her coat and followed Bigger, struggling with the sleeves as she went.

"Topsy Tiddles!" Small groaned. No time to rush to the hay loft or the dark slope above the dairy roof. The others were already downstairs and out the doors. Small dashed into the drawing room, rammed Topsy up the chimney and followed the others to school in agony.

Aunt had just arrived from the south. It was one of our summer grey days; the afternoon turned cold. Aunt demanded a fire in the drawing room.

When halfway home, rain commenced to spit. Small knew what would happen and ran all the way.

It was as she thought it would be. The Elder was just putting the match. Aunt was coughing.

"That chimney needs cleaning!" Small told them.

"Aunt, Mother is calling you like anything, don't you hear?"

To the Elder: "Your Tom Turkey has flown the fence and is making off!"

Both women hurried away. Small was on her knees before the grate.

"You nasty tormenting little beast Topsy! You're no good and now I've told three lies just for you, ugh!"

She rammed the Topsy book into the midst of the flames. That was the end of Topsy Tiddles.

FATHER AND THE MOON

Father and the moon seem part of each other as I remember that night, and both seem to belong to the night, and so did I. Father had taken us on a steamer for an excursion. The steamer ran onto a rock off Cadboro Bay. We were stuck there for hours hoping the high tide would float us off. When it did not, and the night got late, we were put ashore in row boats. Cadboro Bay was a three mile walk from the town; our home was one mile further still. Four miles, and I was only four years old. A long walk for short fat little legs.

A great moon made night almost as light as day. Father held my hand and we led the way. The others were behind. The road was long and steep. The greater part of the road had trees on both sides, and on the end of the long way was the big round moon. Hand in hand Father and I trudged straight towards the moon and talked about it as we went.

"Doesn't she shine? Isn't she round? How soon will we catch up to her, Father?"

"Some while yet. Getting tired?"

"No. If we touch her, when we catch up, will she burn us?"

"I think not. Would you like to be carried a little?"

"No, I am big. I wish my legs were long as yours, then we could take long, long steps together. Do you think moon gets tired?"

"I suppose, having no legs, she rolls."

"That must be easier than walking, mustn't it Father?"

"We will ask moon about that when we catch up. I tell you something, we have a long way to go, but nothing like as far as the moon has."

"Poor moon, she will be so tired."

"Mother will be very anxious, do you think you could go a little faster?"

"Uh, huh, but I am sleepy."

"If moon would yawn as wide as that she would break in two."

"Aha, poor moon. Can't yawn for fear she split. I rather be me than the moon."

GARDENS

At the back of our old home garden were two giant squares of orchard, one of pear, one of cherry trees, each square as big as a city lot. Between was a long, long asparagus bed, and there was spare land flanked by a gravel walk. This spare strip of earth was cut into the children's gardens. Each child could do exactly what he liked in our own garden. It was unsupervised, the most independent spot of our lives.

Bigger's was always trim. She had an English lavender bush, some fine cowslip and polyanthus roots, mignonette and pansies. A dirt path trodden hard by the children's feet divided Bigger's garden from Middle's.

Middle's garden was more cemetery than flower bed. Up near the asparagus bed was a bush of old man's beard[1] and a root of bleeding heart. There was a rim of annuals around the edge of the plot and some seedy-looking pansies. The centre of the plot was bumpy from the shallow graves of creatures buried in shoe boxes, matchboxes and some in paper bags. Creatures as big as cats took an apple box and a grave that took days to dig. It was hard for the three toy spades,

1. Old man's beard: *plant with plumed seedheads, probably* Clematis vitabla *also know as traveller's joy.*

even at work in combination, to dig graves deep enough. Middle tried to combine the planting of a corpse with the simultaneous planting of a flower root to lessen digging. The flowers did not thrive on boxes and died before their roots could reach the meat of the corpse.

Small's garden was at the end of the gravel walk. It was square and small. Everyone walked over it to save the corner. You might as well try to dig cement, and Small's spade was wood. Small gave up flower growing and established a mud pie bakery. Small's spade of wood was blunt. It would not even dent the hard soil till she hit it with a stone. After a number of prodigious grunts, Small gave up and imported dough earth from the chicken yard for her bakery. She made pies of all sizes and shapes but unfortunately, though she stood them in rows on boards, they never even sun-cracked because no sun ever touched Small's garden. "Oh," wailed Small, "if there were only cracks like grown-up pies to let the jam run out, I could bear it."

Brother Dick was too young for a garden then. But by and by when he grew big enough, and Bigger outgrew a child's garden and interested herself in the grown-up garden beds, Small was promoted to Bigger's plot and Dick had Small's.

By and by the three little girls grew up and the town grew up, and the Father and Mother died. Then the old property was divided, cut up into city lots. The Elder built a big house on her lot to rent out but lived on in the family home. Bigger lived with Elder. She did not build a house, she built a garden on her lot next door to the Elder's lot. Middle built her school just opposite and Small an apartment house just round the corner. All staying by Father's original land, the sisters dined together on Sundays immediately after morning

Church. When dinner was over they went to the three houses to inspect the three gardens each had made according to her taste.

Bigger's was the finest of the three, and she was very proud of it. It took up the whole deep lot and had pergolas and rockeries and a vegetable garden and orchard as well as flowers. It took a long time to see it all, for Bigger made us compare each Sunday how much each plant had grown during the week.

Then we crossed the street to Middle's schoolhouse, with a flower and fruit garden behind and a gravel play-yard with a swing for the children. In front it was not so orderly as Bigger's but it was pretty and homey and full of life. "Now," said Small, quivering to show the others what she had made out of her hummocky wild lot. But Bigger said, "I must get ready for Sunday school," and Middle said, "I must take the children to the beach." So Small went to her garden alone.

It was the same every Sunday. Her sisters took no more interest in Small's garden than they had taken in her mud pie bakery. It hurt Small but with a toss of her head she lied, "I don't care. I think mine the very nicest garden of them all," and she opened the gate that shut the apartment house business from her own private garden. There in the cherry tree sat the little monkey Woo with a whoop of joy at seeing her, and there came the great silver Persian cat, and the moment she opened the yard gates, in poured the "Bobbies", adult dogs and puppies. Any kind of creature Small had in her possession at the moment came running to the lawn, for this was their garden as much as Small's. Every flower, every shrub and bulb was a live friend. Today was Small's, her own. The tenants minded their own business on Sundays. And Small had her garden and her creatures.

"Punk," whispered Small into the ear of the great Bobtail kennel sire. "Punk, we have the most lovely garden in the whole world!" and every creature bounced with the truth of it.

Bigger passed by with a tangle of Sabbath School girls hanging on each arm. Middle passed with a drove of infants in wheeling wagons before her and behind her. But Small and her creatures drowsed in their own garden. A nose, a paw touched Small's hammock, or a warm human monkey hand swung the hammock rope. Sway, sway, "Life is dear," sighed Small, and slept a little and sang a little.

SWOONING RHODA

We played ladies with a girl called Rhoda. There were six little girls, three in Rhoda's family and three in ours. So we could have a father, a mother, two children (a good one and a bad one) and a visitor or a servant. But the only one of us who could act a first-rate mock swoon was Rhoda. She had a colourless pale face and was lean, with a faraway, languishing look in her eyes. Standing, sitting or lying, Rhoda could fold herself with elegant swaying motion and sink prone. The difficulty was to think up tragic situations worthy of swoons.

Sometimes we played ladies in Rhoda's back field, sometimes on the rocky ridge behind our cow pasture. In both places we had delicious make-believe houses: no walls, no boundaries. Perhaps that is what the many heavenly mansions will be like.

Our houses always had to have a drawing room and a kitchen and a front door bell. Those were the rooms in which our play activities took place. The visiting ladies were always very elegant and the cook gruff. The kitchen was the loveliest room of all, a big separate rock covered with deep green moss. A little gully divided it from the drawing room. Cook had to either jump the gully or shout, "Dinner do be hot on the plates, mum!"

Rhoda was always a grand lady. She chose the name of Mrs. Cholmondy. To be sure, when cook rushed in, shouting, "Excuse me Mrs. Cholmondy, your child has pot drowned he in the kitchen sink!" Rhoda looked round to be sure the spot where she was going to stretch her lank length had no sticks nor stones to scratch her as she sprawled at rigid length and moaned, while we chafed her hands. Two fanned and cook rushed off to an imaginary tap in the spirea bush with a rusty can to fetch water.

When somebody held the rusty can to Rhoda's lips she usually revived enough to sit up and take notice before the water splashed. Everyone said, "Oh Rhoda, that swoon was a beauty."

Though the rest of us practiced we could only flop and get bruised. Had anyone succeeded like Rhoda, we would have felt they had infringed on her patent.

YELLOW SCUM

Mother was proud of our dairy. The milk bucket and pans shone like the sun. Old cow was a great red and white spotted beast that gave quantity, but the little Jersey gave quality. The cream was leather thick. Bong[1] brought in the great shining bucket brimming with the warm foamy milk and set it on the kitchen table. A piece of cloth was placed over the wire strainer and the milk was poured into great round pans. These were in turn set into a greater pan containing boiling water and put on top of the stove to scald. Mother knew just in how many minutes the cream crinkled up like bad sewing. This was Devonshire cream, used on porridge or deep apple pie or on junket for the children's tea. And sometimes, if I was lucky enough to wiggle my seat at breakfast so that the red tea cozy was between my plate and Father's eye, Mother substituted the hated porridge for a slice of bread and cream.

Brother Dick was a skinny, fragile little boy, and instead of ordering him tonics, Dr. Helmcken would order two tablespoons full of cream every morning. There was nothing skinny or fragile about me. I used to hang around the dairy door, hoping.

1. Bong *came to work for the Carr family from China at the age of twelve. He was part of the household thoughout Emily's childhood.*

One morning at cream time, two little city boys were playing in our yard with Dick. Mother, thinking to give them a treat, creamed them all round. They made dreadful faces and went running home to their mother. They told her the Carrs' milk had the most disgusting thick yellow scum on it and was quite unlike the nice blue kind their milkman brought them. Their mother thought it a joke, and told our mother, who sent her a jar of yellow scum.

CONFIRMATION

Laying her hand on me, Mother said to her old friend the Bishop, seated by her bedside, "All my children but this one and the little brother have been received into the Church. I shall not be here when they are old enough for Confirmation. You will see that it is attended to when the right time comes, Bishop?"

"Ah, indeed my friend, it is a sacred trust."

Even Confirmation itself did not seem to me at the moment as sacred as Mother's trust in the Bishop and the Bishop's promise to Mother who was dying.

Two years had passed since Mother's death. I do not think that the Bishop had spoken to me since. They lived opposite us; we often met but he passed with only a nod.

Elder said, "You are to attend the Confirmation class this year, after school on Fridays, don't forget."

Six lanky girls waited in the old Sunday School room beside the church next Friday after school. Boys met on a different day. I was not a very enthusiastic member of the class; we had between four and five miles walking every day for school. However I remembered the Bishop's promise to my mother and I felt the smirk of the privileged. I would be a sort of guest of honour in the class, because Mother had put me specially in the Bishop's care about Confirmation. Surely he would remember this child, now that I was under his nose in his class.

We sat on crude benches, waiting for the Bishop. I soon found there was nothing to be smart about or to feel special about. The Bishop did not seem to remember me; to be sure, he kept his eyes shut all the time. When he opened them, it was to give each of the six girls their questions, then he shut them again and waited for the six answers. Each girl took her question and wrassled with it. It was difficult to tell if the Bishop was asleep or awake. He and the flies tagged along together in a dreary hum, and the hot sun blazed in through the windowless blinds.

Finally we did get through the course and we were running through it for final rehearsal. Things were going badly with me at home, the same old troubles—these miserable remittance people from the old country with whom the Elder would fill our house. I was not nice to them, and after a severe attack of rebellion, my sister the Elder said, "Now Miss Impertinence, you walk straight out the door and over to the Bishop's house. Tell him I say you are far too wicked to be confirmed and are to drop out from the class."

It wanted two weeks to the Confirmation Sunday. The others in the class would wonder. All of us were sewing on our white Confirmation dresses. The Elder could not have thought of a plan to hurt me more. I walked slowly up the Bishop's driveway. Its curves hid the study window. Laurel trees and little bushes of yellow roses grew all the way up the drive. I always stopped to smell them; this day I did not. There seemed no sweetness anywhere.

The Bishop's wife opened the door. I loved her. She gave me kisses, a dozen in a cluster, and made to lead me into the sitting-room. I had never been inside the Bishop's study before. My feet stopped outside the door, clumsy with fear.

"I want, at least, I have got to see the Bishop." The old lady was surprised, but she opened the door of the study and stood aside.

The study was a small room littered with papers and boxes. The Bishop sat at a table drawn close to the fire. The Bishop's wife left the room and I stood there before the closed eyelids of the Bishop. He had forgotten me, so I made a little fidget. "Ah, child," but there was no recognition in his voice. The pen was still between his fingers—perhaps that was one of his sermons on love and charity before him. He gave a deep, almost patient sigh, as if I were one of life's crosses, and repeated, "Well, child!" with slight asperity.

"I'm Small, Mr. Bishop. You remember, you used to come see my mother before she died?"

"Indeed I remember Emily Carr. A good Christian woman. What can I do for her daughter, Small they call you don't they?"

"I'm wicked sir, and my sister sent me to say I was not fit for Confirmation and was to drop out of the class."

"I am sorry to hear you are bad."

"Not horrible badness, sir, not stealing or lying or things like that, just rebellion and impertinence." Then I tumbled choking into an orgy of tears.

Having expected major wickedness, the Bishop sighed and laid his pen down and crossed his hands. "You are young yet. It would not hurt to wait another year."

Had he no suggestion, no help to offer, no questions to ask?

Every moment my heart grew harder towards the Bishop and towards his religion.

The Bishop's eyes were closed again. I glanced towards the door. It was not latched. Turning, I crept quickly.

In a few steps I was through the hall and out in the open. I scuttled behind the gracious laurels' shelter. The little yellow roses never smelled so sweet. I stopped to smell each bush.

All my school companions were confirmed that year. They had wondered why I dropped out of the class. I was confirmed the next year. It did not mean much to me, not what it had meant the first time I joined the class.

THE OLD ROSEWOOD PIANO

It was a pretty old instrument of rosewood that came from England in the same ship with Father and Mother. The piano was an upright with open fretwork over pink silk. It had a pair of brass candle holders in brackets that swung and rattled furiously when the Elder played, and it had two carved front legs and a piano stool that spun and was done in leather. Our piano smelled of furniture polish and housed us all in its reflections.

We were not a musical family. My eldest sister was the only one who performed. Bigger, Middle and I each had a month or two of lessons to try us out. Our teacher decided it was not worthwhile for us to continue.

The piano had always been around. I do not know who taught the Elder music; it must have been a specialist in loudness. You'd wonder how the little piano could stand it. We always had hymns Sunday night, each one choosing. Besides this, the Elder played the "Maiden's Prayer with Variations", which meant that the maiden shouted her requests, or snivelled them out in tremolo or she threatened dictatorially, bullied and cajoled. She always ended with a bang, as if to say, "There you are, God! Take it or leave it. You told us to ask and I have." She also played somebody's daughter, a miller, a farmer or something and assorted bars from a number of other pieces.

The Elder also accompanied my future brother-in-law who vocalled in tremolo. My future brother-in-law was unpleasantly impressive when he stood beside our little piano to sing. It looked so much more a lady than he did standing beside its rosy fretwork. He was smug and trimmed up enough, but he—he sang semi-religion and tremoloed like jelly. My pretty sister who was engaged to him sat close clasping her hands and rolling her eyes, generally holding one of his hands while he sang. The other he thrust between the buttons of his tight black frock coat with long clerical skirts. He parted his hair in the middle; it curled and his mustache stuck out both sides of his head like a pair of buffalo horns. They were waxed stiff and he took his hand from my sister's periodically to twirl it, which muffled the groaning of his low notes—which became so low and unmusical they sounded like anchors thrown overboard and drowned. The Elder filled in the long moaning pauses with variations from the Maiden's Prayer.

The Elder did not approve of sweethearting and insisted that my sister and future brother-in-law keep to the sofa well in the background, crowding us four younger children up to the keyboard and telling us to keep our eyes on the hymn book. We knew it was so that we should not see the lovemaking. The wise old piano blinked and winked her candles in their sconces as if trying to keep tears back.

Poor old piano, you did not know much about love, nobody coaxed soft tender tones out of you, as I have seen musicians coax sweetness out of pianos much uglier, much clumsier than you. At last your tinkle got very, very weak and feeble. Then you had outlived all the family except Middle and me who did not piano-play, but to whom fell the sad job of cleaning out the old home.

They carted you away to the auction-rooms. I expect your insides were taken out and you are now a cabinet or a bureau in a drawing room or antique shop. I expect even as a cupboard you were elegant.

I expect your most elegant moment was when Father and Mother had you boxed and you set out for the New World. This is the new world you came to, all round Cape Horn in company with Father and Mother, their two daughters, a pair of dapple grey horses, the big tin roasting screen, the mangle and garden roller that had nearly as much clank and clatter in her insides as you.

SMALL'S FIRST LOCK AND KEY

"I hope your husband beats you, Small!"

Small was sixteen, the Elder thirty-two. They faced each other glowering. Small had asked for possession of a small locked travelling bag that was her own by right. The Elder refused, and Small turned impertinent.

"Any husband who tries beating me is going to look like a fly that writhed over a sticky fly paper all night. The bag is mine. I want it! It was bought for me to hold my luggage on my first trip to Puget Sound[1]. It is doing nothing up there on that top shelf, only holding its own emptiness. I want it to lock away something very particular. I mean to have it, so there! You are saying no just for meanness."

"What can you have so particularly private that it needs a lock and key?"

"None of your business."

The Elder made a lunge towards Small's ear and missed because of Small's quick dodge. She dare not strike more than an ear of Small now.

1. At age twelve, Emily travelled with a family friend to Puget Sound, while recovering from typhoid fever. The trip is mentioned in The Book of Small, in the chapter "Ways of Getting Round."

"Next time you hit, I hit back," Small had told her a year ago, when she was fifteen.

Small was writing poetry, that was what she wanted to lock up. She knew as poetry it was poor; that was not why she wanted to hide it. She was writing from her heart; that was why she wanted to write and to hide it. She wrote as an outlet, a relief. She had tried writing deeper than she could talk. She wrote about jugs and frogs and love and dying and religion. If anyone saw her thoughts and ridiculed her poems, she would die of shame. That is why she wanted the bag. Her boxes and her bureau drawers were still under strict supervision for tidiness. Small was not neat. That key would be such a comfort.

Small pushed a chair under the shelf, climbed, reached the bag, glanced across her shoulder at the angry Elder and made a face. Then drawing the key from its lock, she slipped it in her pocket, jumped from the chair, and with an insolent nod to the Elder and a pert wriggle at her from the bag, left the room carrying her small gain. That was the first piece of private property over which Small had ever had control.

The Elder's long forefinger wagged at the girl's retreating figure. Again she called, "I hope he beats you, hard."

"Shan't worry till he comes," Small retorted. "I s'pose the more he beats me the more I'll adore him, because I was just born contrary." That's the worst of it, she thought.

SNOB CHILDREN

We were child snobs. It was not exactly our fault nor was it the fault of our parents. Snobbery was thrust upon us, but it was a pity all the same, and I look back on those years of my school life with a certain amount of shame.

This was the way of it. When we were young, the Canadian Public School system was young too. The ultra-English people in the Crown Colony of British Columbia could not accept what they still insisted on calling "Free School Education" for their children. The silly things could not be made to see that they were paying for it in taxes. There were a few small high-priced private schools which taught little but snobbery and good manners. Those who could afford it, sent their children home to England to be "finished." They came back very uppish and airy.

Father did not send his two oldest daughters to England. He finished them in Victoria in private schools but was not satisfied at the results. It was really Mother who finished her little girls. After they were finished, Father had a nice long rest from education problems because the three little boys who were born died before they needed educating. His youngest three daughters and their little brother Dick all stayed in the nursery till my eldest sister had taught them the elements of reading, writing and arithmetic.

But the time came—Bigger and Middle must go further. My legs lacked length and strength for the four mile walk every day, most up hill at that, to the Girls' Public Central School. Father took a bold plunge. None of our friends sent their children to the Public School. Mother saw him pack Bigger and Middle off to the Public School with tears in her eyes. She wanted to keep her little girls' manners gentle; to have them grow up gentlewomen. Their manners would have a good deal of knocking about in the Public School of those days. There were some rough uncouth children from many countries whose parents had migrated to Canada to swell their own importance and to create a place in the world for their children. Dick was sent to an old lady famed for grounding boys well. I was sent to a nearby school for little girls till I should be stronger and more sensible in my pick of companions.

Those of our friends who sent their children to Victoria's "private schools for girls", schools that skimped learning and specialized in good manners, shook their heads and watched for the Carr girls' manners to deteriorate.

Mother had gently pleaded, "Richard, must our children mingle with the uncouth?"

Father said, "This is the New World."

"Keep aloof, be courteous, be kind but keep aloof. Give all your attention to your books, and don't mix," Mother told us.

We carried our lunch with us but were not allowed to eat it with the other children. Instead we had to walk a half-mile and eat it in my married sister's garden. With the return half-mile, that made five miles a day we walked. When I joined my two sisters at the public school, I used to sit down on some rocks on the edge of Beacon Hill Park, from where I could see our church, and cry for tiredness most days.

I loathed school. I think the root of my loathing was planted in weariness at that long, long walk, and then there was arithmetic. I drew pigs and donkeys all over my textbooks. The pigs I labelled "arithmetic" and the donkeys "Emily Carr."

Mother's anxious eyes were on our manners. Father's quick ear was alive to any faulty speech, any slang. Is it not surprising that we came through teen-age prigs? Snobby as peacocks in a goose pen? The next generation, our own nieces included, came through better. They weren't being watched and warned all the time.

After we had been going to Public School for several months, a prominent doctor in the town came to my father. He said, "Mr. Carr, what do you think of the Public School? I hear you are sending your girls there. I have a daughter to educate."

Father said, " The Public School is good. My daughters are working for teacher certificates."

The doctor sent his daughter. More and more people began sending daughters. Soon only a few snobby old stick-in-a-muds called it the Free School.

The snob soon rubbed off us. Hail to the pioneer parents who had to make the first break!

ADOPTION

I had been grown up many years before it came to me with full force what Mother did for me by not giving me away. Both ladies who wanted me were dead; either would have left me well off. My own mother was dead, too, but I had been mothered by her till I was twelve.[1] That was worth more than the other ladies' money.

In Vancouver I met a young woman who had a most attractive little girl. The girl took painting lessons from me and I got to know mother and daughter intimately. One day as I was talking enthusiastically to the woman about her child, she confided to me:

"My present husband is not her father. I have been married twice. The first time I was very young. I married for money and because I was unhappy at home. The man was twice my age. Three months after our marriage he was killed in a driving accident. The accident of course was a great shock to me, not his death. I tried to act the mournful young widow but I had not loved him.

"In due time my little girl was born, a tiny child, premature and very small. My doctor advised, 'Leave the baby with the nuns. Go

---

1. *Her mother died in 1886, when Emily was fourteen. However, during the last two years of Mother's illness she was bedridden, and the Elder (Edith) took over all responsibility for guiding the younger children and running the household.*

abroad right away. It is the best chance for both of you.' I put Eva in care of the convent nuns and travelled. I was very well off. I could go where I pleased. I travelled for six years, then I came back to my child. She was tiny, tiny, the most perfect little thing you ever saw, fragile but healthy.

"Soon I met an engineer and fell in love with him. By marrying him I forfeited my fortune. He adopted my child and gave her his name. My second husband was not a rich man, but he held good positions; he was higher management at mines. I followed him, living in company towns. We lived comfortably on his salary in houses provided for managers.

"The free life was just the thing for Eva. Sun, air, riding, boating, she became if not robust, at least normal in size and normally healthy. We were generally within reach of large cities and my husband, Eva's adopted father, gave her a liberal education. Had he been unable to do so and if anyone with money had offered to adopt and educate her, I should have given her up. I should have felt it my duty."

I replied, "To give your child away? To give that lovely girl away! I thought you were devoted to her?"

"That is why I would not have stood between her and education."

"Oh, could education or any other thing have compensated for the love and care of her own mother?"

"I think so," she said.

"I do not!" and Mother, my Mother! Thank God you did not.

The toys were laid away for remembrance, and taken out often to be looked at and fondled. Mrs. Bales allowed me to finger some toy patty-pans and a little wooden rolling pin belonging to her dead child.

The woman stooped and touched my hair. "Fair like my child's. Soft as silk," she said. Then she went on talking earnestly to my mother.

I had not noticed before what they were talking about. They now apparently took up where they had left off when she came and got out the toys and bent to touch my hair.

"Just the same age as my own; you have three small girls Mrs. Carr, three little steps . . . this fat little one now . . . spare her to me. I could give her everything. She would be well off when we died."

I had heard these same words before. Where? I remember Mother told me that another woman who wanted Mother to give me to her had said, "I have three boys but no daughter. Give me that one —Oh please—You have two more little steps."

My mother's answer was, "I could not spare one of my children."

Mother bade me, "Get up," and she hugged me so fiercely it almost hurt.

"Run into the garden and play," she said, "I will be coming in a minute." I went, leaving the two ladies alone.

When they came from the house both ladies had been crying. Mother held the other woman's hand and patted it. They kissed which was unusual.

Mother called to me, "Come!"

"Kiss Mrs. Bales and hug her," she whispered to me, and I did. Then we went home.

FATHER'S TEMPER

I believe that Father enjoyed his tempers. I am not sure but that the rest of the family did not rather like them too. Seems to me our young life would have been rather flat without them. It kept us alive, having to jump right and left to obey his terse orders, to scuttle away to do his bidding and to control our own wishes in subservience to his. Mother's drawing room lady friends, Dick's backyard boy friends all faded by way of back fences and front door at the casual remark from afar: "Father's coming."

If Father did come in unawares and catch some of us entertaining, he was never rude to the people but his manner was stiff and cold and plainly intimated: "This bit of the earth is mine, trespassers must take consequences. This is my house, my garden, my wife, my children." Our friends respected the invisible scrawl over everything inside the Carr's gate: "Keep out. This means you." Father was busy in his castle.

When Father had the gout, that was the time for even the family to fade. We all did whatever we could to alleviate his pain but even Mother fell back before his wraths. I believe gout is a great agony and the temper is attacked as well as the body.

Some things one learns by instinct. One is "Don't worry a gout patient!"

Old Doctor Helmcken understood. All the way upstairs he'd shout "How is Carr today? How's his temper?" And he would walk into the room, give Father a little kind bullying and some very nasty medicine that turned Father from fierce to very low-spirited, so that his temper all leaked away in tears. It was horrible to see Father cry! We would all rather have the scorch of his temper.

Mother would say, "I can't bear to see him so downhearted, Doctor."

Then the old Doctor would pat her shoulder and reply, "There, there, lass, if he wasn't crying he'd be cursing."

"My husband has never cursed," Mother would say a little stiffly.

At the front door, just before Doctor put the match to a new cigar he was chewing the end off, he would double back to the bedroom. Pretending he had left his hat in Father's room, though Mother saw, and he knew, it was in his hand all the time. His shaggy head was thrust in the door of my Father's room.

"A bit of a cuss wouldn't hurt you, Carr. It'd do you good." Then the Doctor ran downstairs, lit his cigar and was off. But in all my life I never heard my Father use one oath nor curse.

Well, after an attack of gout everyone was so glad when Father began to get fierce again, shouting, "Are the gates shut? Have you children got things all over the garden that should be in your playroom? Have you looked after this? Have you done that?"

Everyone hopped around doing his bidding. His food pleased him once more, though it could not have been better for the care we put on it, but that he enjoyed it again.

One ordinary thing that particularly annoyed Father's temper was some table mats that Mother had to keep the hot dishes from whitening the polish on the dining table. If I set the table I was always careful to put them on. It was such fun to see them fly over our heads and the dining table and arrive before the fire, sailing high, falling heavy. Whoever sat nearest the fender[1] got up quietly without being told and picked the mats up before they scorched. The whole scene was over in about two minutes but the hot dish had marred the table for the rest of the week. The whole family patiently rubbed stuff in that takes the white hot mark from the polished wood.

"Dear old table mats you were good sports. It was wonderful what usage you stood!" They were made of a coarse green grass-like reed, sewn together with scarlet thread and came from China.

1. Fender: *a metal guard, frame or screen in front of a fireplace to keep sparks from the room.*

DECEMBER BIRTHDAY

I have always been ashamed of my birthday because it came too near Christmas. Everybody thought they had their Christmas money nicely apportioned, and then came the wretched 13th of December and the wretched little Small's Birthday! And somebody's present had to be pinched to make allowance for it. When the thirteenth itself came, everyone was rushing and had no time for a picnic, a party or anything special even if the weather would have permitted. Which, being midwinter, it never did.

But there is one happy thing that Mother never forgot. The Christmas puddings were all made and hanging in a row by their tails under the pantry shelf. On the last nail hung a tiny "sample" pudding cooked in a great Delft[1] tea cup. This sample pudding was made specially to be eaten on my birthday. Mother never forgot. We all passed judgement on the quality of the great one to be eaten on Christmas day. I was not greatly fond of Christmas pudding but Mother remembering my birthday "sample" pudding specially like that made up for everything. It seemed the beginning wonderfulness of all birthdays.

1. Delft: *a name now used for any blue-and-white glazed earthenware pottery. It was originaly made in the town of* Delft *in Holland during the 17th century.*

FIRST SNOW

That morning, even the cozy warmth of our house felt different, even to my youngness it did. Everything was quite still and whited. Everyone looked out of the windows. "It is beautiful!" they said, "beautiful, white and clean," but shivered in saying it and held their hands by the fire as they said it. The world had smothered her noises. It was like a stopped clock. Those who came in from the outside were rubbing their hands; their skin was red and cold to touch.

"It is getting quite deep," they said, stamping the white stuff off their shoes by the fire. The white stuff turned to little puddles as it warmed.

"What is it, Father," I asked, putting my finger into a snow puddle.

"Snow, you silly!"

"Old Mother Holle[1] is plucking her geese for Christmas, somebody told me."

"What silly things they tell children!"

"Father, what is it really? I know the feel of feathers, and they don't melt."

1. Old Mother Holle, *also called "Mother Hulda" a character found in one of* Grimm's Fairy Tales.

"Snow, snow!" he answered.

I ate a handful. "Snow, snow what are you? You come from the sky, why aren't you blue?"

Boys and girls were passing to Beacon Hill dragging sleds and snowballing.

Bigger and Middle knew everything about this snow stuff; they were always two and four years ahead of me. The wind was rough and growled round corners. The sky was dark against the white earth. The air was full of this scurrying and whirling snow stuff that was not goose down. The flakes bumped and tumbled against each other seeing who could hit earth first. They could not steer at all, and, if there was a tree or roof or telephone wire in the way they had to sit down on that and wait till the wind came and set them going again.

The white earth would not let night come down and kept dark up in the sky that night. When Father came home from town, it was still sort of day, sunless daylight.

"Snow, snow, Father what is snow?"

Father did not believe in fairy tales. He told deeper than I could follow.

"Take me out, Father, I want to feel the snow."

Mother put a knitted red wool hood on me and long black wool grown-up stockings on top of my shoes and gartered[2] neck high, anyway as high as I sat. Bigger and Middle watched but did not want to come out. They knew the feel of snow; they watched from the window, giggling. When the front door opened, a troop of snow-flakes rushed in, but the big hall stove sent them to nowhere.

2. *Garters were used to hold stockings up. The stockings would have been pulled up to the very top of her legs, not her neck.*

"Don't let's go down the path where everyone goes. Let's go where it is smooth and deep. Let's go over to a new clean world where your best flowers are asleep. Wouldn't it be fun to go walking right over your best flower bed and not hurt a thing?"

"All right," said Father. We tramped right across where his best hyacinths grew. My feet sank down and down till my legs were planted as deep as my black over-stockings came up. My skirts spread out on top of the snow like umbrellas.

"Father, I'm planted, my legs can't lift! The snow is too high for me to step over. I think we'd better go home now. Let's go home, Father."

"How so? I thought you wanted to go all round Beacon Hill?" laughed Father.

"Not just now. Let's wait till summer?"

THE SPOTTED DOG

I walked down Government Street with my mother. Government Street was the most important street of the little town of Victoria. I didn't reach up to Mother's shoulder.

Presently I saw a running dog, yellow with black spots, racing towards us from the outskirts of the town. He came fast and straight; I thought he was lost. When within a few feet of me, he stopped and looked straight into my face. I looked back into his. Then he raised himself and put a paw on each of my shoulders. He licked my face. Mother screamed. She always feared strange dogs.

Several people stopped to ask, "Did the dog bite the little girl?"

"No," said my mother, "but I thought he was going to."

I leaned back against my mother to steady the dog's weight.

"Shoo! Go away!" she said, but I threw my arms around his neck and kept him for a moment.

I do not know where he came from, where he went to, or to whom he belonged, but for that moment, he was my dog. The first I had owned. He introduced me to entire dogdom, and for that I love him still.

THE LITTLEST BRIDESMAID

There was to be a wedding, the first in the family. Everyone was in a twitter. Bigger, Middle and Small were to be bridesmaids. Small had no idea what a wedding was all about.[1] Pretty Tallie was crying her eyes out because Bishop Cridge had been detained up north and would not be back on time to do it, so a strange clergyman was to be brought in. What "it" was, Small had no idea except that the drawing room was all decorated with flowers, great sprays of mock-orange blossom which smelled wonderful. A marvellous three-story cake had come from town. It had a pair of clasped hands on top made of hard stuff (it wasn't even sweet to taste—Small tried) and a pair of tiny doves floating on squiggly springs made of sugar on top of the hands. This marvellous affair sat on the centre of the dining room table, which was pulled out the extent of all its leaves and then some, so that there was only just room to squeeze behind the end chairs.

The wedding was to take place on the first of June. The day was fine. In the morning, Tallie the bride did something none of us had ever dared to do before: went to the not-quite-ripe cherry tree

1. *Emily was ten and a half years old at the time; Clara (Tallie), the bride, married Major John Nicholles in 1882, at age 24.*

without permission of the head of the family, gathered a handful of cherries and ate them.

When we asked how Tallie dared help herself before the tree was pronounced ripe, Big Sister said, "Tallie will not have to obey Father and Mother any more now. She is going to be married and she will have to obey her husband." She was going with this husband to live in a home of her own. It was all very extraordinary, particularly about the cherries; Father's command had always been so strict about that.

However, the bustle and excitement were very pleasant. We had the loveliest new white dresses to bridesmaid in, new sashes, hair ribbons, white shoes, gloves and stockings.

The strange parson came at eight o'clock and all the guests. Mother looked lovely; I don't know that she had what people call beauty. She was small, dark-haired and gentle. I know now she was full of the beauty of kindness and motherliness. Father looked wretched. He did not like giving up any of his daughters; besides he hated the drawing room furniture.

The chairs and sofa were beautiful shapes; they were mahogany and upholstered in horsehair. But they had an unhappy arrangement of castors, and if you did not sit just the way they thought you ought, they tipped you onto the floor. Father suffered two or three tips, and he could not bear to look foolish, so he took a dining room cane-seat chair into the drawing room with him for the wedding. He never moved more than four inches away from it, for fear someone else would prefer it to horsehair, too, and he would have to stand or be tipped.

We youngsters were dressed early and then all the grown-ups went up to dress the bride. We were told to take the greatest care to keep clean, and we sat in a row in the decorated drawing room admiring everything.

Suddenly Small remembered the ducks were not shut up for the night. Like a whirl she was off, tearing through the yard. By the ditch in the corner there was a plank. It was slippery, and down she went in the mud. The side of the overskirt of the new dress was looped up with ribbon and a bunch of pink roses and white ribbon. Now it was a sight!

Small let out a wail. "Oh the wedding can't be now, the wedding can't be! They'll all be so mad with me because the wedding can't be. What shall I do? What shall I do? I've broken the wedding!"

"What is the uproar, Small?" Bigger crossed the yard and looked. "Oh you dirty child! The wedding will go on all right, don't alarm yourself. Only you won't be there, though, and I doubt if you get any wedding cake . . . afterward either. You'll be in bed for the wedding."

Small stopped bellowing. "She can't be married without brides-maids, can she?" Small asked in a scared whisper.

"There's Middle and me."

"Doesn't there have to be three? Oh I wanted so much to see how it was done."

"Well, I guess all the wedding you will see or hear is the clatter of the supper dishes from your bed. Now I'm going in to tell Mother about you."

Small picked herself up and followed. At the kitchen door they met the Bishop's wife.

"Poor lamb, poor lamb!"

She kissed Small's tear-soaked cheek between her hands. Usually Small resented those little "hundreds and thousand" kisses that Mrs. Cridge scattered over her face as sun scatters freckles, but tonight, she found them infinitely comforting. The Bishop's wife took her to the kitchen sink. She sent Bigger for half a dozen clean towels. She soaped and ironed and scrubbed. There was more ribbon upstairs and more rosebuds in the garden.

Middle said, "Keep the hurt side close to me," and held Small's hand tight.

They were bringing the bride downstairs now, the lovely bride! Small was quite forgotten and the wedding proceeded.

CONSCIENCE

Middle and Small sat on the edges of the two wooden chairs in their father's office. Customers sat there when they came to give huge wholesale orders for groceries, while Father sat writing the orders in his book. The little girls' legs dangled. The chairs were designed for the big. The outer office and the outer store were very still. The only live things in the whole place were the children, the cats, and the fire in the office stove.

The children had brought their father a crock of hot soup for his lunch. It was his first day downtown after an attack of gout. Having eaten, Father said, "I have to go up to Government Street. I shall be gone a quarter of an hour, the men are away at lunch. You children take charge of the office, say I will be back in fifteen minutes, but nobody comes at lunch time."

The children did not talk. Each was busy with her own thoughts. There was nothing to talk about. Opposite them were four shelves on which stood glass sample jars of English candies. Even the shiny jars with their wide mouths and glass stoppers invited silence and secrecy. When ladies wholesaled sweets for their children (English ladies who believed that there were no wholesome candies in the world except those made in England), Father unstopped the bottles and the ladies dipped with their long slim fingers, though the jars were quite wide-mouthed enough to admit the whole hand.

Small slipped off the chair's edge. Without her even suggesting it to her feet, they just crossed the short few steps to her father's wicker office chair. It creaked when she climbed into it, and a muffled blotting paper tap or two told that Small's feet were standing on Father's blotting pad, on the office table. Middle kept her eyes averted.

Three clinks of three glass stoppers, a pause between each, again father's chair creaked. The cat yelled as Small stepped on her tail in dismounting from the chair. Small soothed the cat and then sat demurely down on the edge of the yellow chair beside Middle. "Here's half."

Middle pocketed one square acid drop, one pink pear drop and one burnt almond.

"Guess it's time for the men to be back from lunch," said Small carelessly.

"Guess it is," said Middle with care, plunging the sweets deep into her pocket.

The men came. They climbed onto their high stools before the higher desk and buried their noses in their ledgers. Then the children's father came back.

"Anybody been?" he asked.

"No, Father."

"Good girls. You shall have candy pay for keeping office."

"No thank you, Father."

"No thank you, Father."

"Hello, what's the matter, shed your sweet teeth?"

"It would spoil our dinner," said Middle.

Father frowned. "I have not seen anything yet that did that."

Then he looked harder still at the crooked mess by the blotter and—a footprint on its clean surface. But he said nothing.

Small and Middle left the store silently but hurriedly. They walked till they had crossed Fort Street and on the other side of the road they had passed the big austere brick Customs House. The Gregories might be working in their little garden in front of their quarters in the Customs House basement.

Between Fort Street and the Post Office lay a stretch of rough land, rocky and unbuilt upon. For the convenience of foot-passers, a sidewalk on trestles had been built over its rocks, two planks wide, and a handrail.

Here the children had to walk singly. Small was ahead. She came to a great knothole in the plank and stopped so dead that Middle nearly fell over her. Slowly Small dipped from her pocket one square acid drop, one pink pear drop and a burnt almond and dropped them through the knothole. Then she leaned on the rail and watched while Middle, too, dropped through the hole one square acid drop, one pink pear drop and a burnt almond. They walked home briskly in silence and ate a hearty dinner.

A DIP AT DAWN

Mrs. Bales had a bath-house of her very own. It stood on stilts right out in the sea in front of the beach at the edge of the Harbour, where Mr. Bales had his Shipyard. The tide came up and filled the bath-house with icy water, then the tide went out again and the bath water emptied out into the sea. Mrs. Bales did not have to turn a tap or pull a plug. The tide pushed water through the wide cracks in the bath-house wall. The tide sucked it back again into the harbour.

Mrs. Bales invited my big sister to spend the night at her house so as to enjoy an early morning dip in her bath-house. She told her to bring me along that I too could dip. It sounded splendid. After our dip we were to breakfast off Mrs. Bales' beautiful buttermilk English muffins with honey from her own bees and butter from her own cow.

Mrs. Bales was nice. She had no children. Her one little girl had died, but she had a room full of canaries all flying loose. The Bales' house stood in a garden on the bank above the shipyard. You went down a path of black dust through the orchard to the beach and bath-house, walking in the shadow of new boats perched up on blocks, boats that had not yet learned to swim. The inside of the Bales' house was rather dark. The rooms were low. All the house smelled of ripe apples.

It seemed as if I had hardly gone to bed before Mrs. Bales and my sister started to try and pull me out of sleep again. One on either side of the bed, they poked and pinched me. Daylight had not quite come. I did not want to wake. I fought them.

By the feel of their hands and by their voices I knew that it was Mrs. Bales and my sister but when I opened my eyes I did not recognize their bodies or their hair. Surprise sat me right up. They were in their bath-suits and their hair was dragged back slick and tight so as to be waterproof. It was so tight that it made their eyes pop and their pigtails stick out straight behind their heads.

Their suits were of serge, Mrs. Bales' green, my sister's navy. They had sailor boy collars trimmed with white braid. Sailor colours reminded me of the sea and of our dip. I shuddered to see that the bath suits were dry and wrinkled. I wished they had dripped and looked wet; then I should have known that the dip was over. To think of sea dips before the sun is up makes one shivery. The ladies looked cold, sour and determined. They were not chirruping about the delight of sea dipping in an unspoiled sea, before work on the harbour started, as they had talked of last night.

Peeling off my gown they stood me naked in the middle of the floor. My sister said, "She can't go in like that!" and Mrs. Bales nodded. I knew they meant that I had far too much pink skin showing.

Mrs. Bales shut her eyes and thought. She always saw her thoughts much clearer when her eyes were shut. Suddenly they opened as if they had seen a vision. "Jimmy's shrunk underwear!" she exclaimed, and darting to a chest, pulled out a great suit of men's underwear. She held it up against me, doubling back the arms and legs, running her fingers through the folds and bending my hands and feet back to feel where my arms and legs ended. Mrs. Bales' eyesight was very poor. The best way for her to see anything was to shut her eyes tight and to roam her fingers over the object.

The shape of Mr. Bales was like a big apple with a small apple for a head. He had very little hair but a lot of smile. Mrs. Bales looked more like a pear. Her face was long, pale and greeny-yellow. The pear's big end was up and covered with heavy brown hair. Her cheeks sagged, falling round to her mouth in flutes edged with a ribbon of pale lips, which wriggled and twisted as she talked. The chin end of the pear was small and perched upon a thin stalky neck. In her green bath-suit Mrs. Bales looked as if the pear tree's entire crop had culminated in one magnificent fruit crowning the tree.

With tight shut eyes she marched across to the bureau, knocked down all the standing up things and felt for the scissors. Darting back with them she lopped off one arm and one leg of Jimmy's underwear at the fold she had made. She then fell to talking to my sister and forgot the other arm and leg, putting away the scissors. "There! Jump in child," she said. "The tide is ready."

My sister did not like to reach for the scissors and finish destroying Mr. Bales' clothes so she rolled back the long arm and the long leg and I climbed in. I could not nearly fill the middle of Mr. Bales' suit so my sister pleated it over me. Then she took the lace out of one of my shoes and tied it round my waist. She took the lace from my other shoe and tied my hair in a bunch behind my head, and knotted the two laces together, which dragged my head back like a horse's check rein.

I complained a little and she said, "Never mind. One lace keeps you from falling out of the suit, the other holds your head up so you won't drown."

We marched downstairs and out into the cold. Now that the sun was rising I could see the whole of both ladies. Above the waist they were all puffs and bulges. Blouses bloused, sleeves puffed to the elbow and then frilled. The serge blouses buttoned clear to their chins under the sailor collars and down to where a waist band kept their full skirts on. The waist band halted the buttons. Below the skirt, bloomers sagged over their knees but were strapped in below, bursting out again in frills which hung half down their calves which were draped in ungartered stockings of black cotton. Everywhere their suits could be ornamented, they were rimmed with rows and rows of white braid.

My sister wore Mrs. Bales' felt slippers. Mrs. Bales wore a pair of Jimmy's boots. Except that the ladies did not wear veils nor gloves, every inch of their skin was covered. How the sea was ever going to find their skins to do them that tremendous amount of good which they talked about last night, no one could imagine. Each carried a bath towel round her head like a muff.

As we started down the dusty path, Mr. Bales' long leg came unrolled and so did his long arm. One flapped and the other dragged, stirring up the dust as I walked behind the others. Mrs. Bales went first, swinging the rusty key, which squeaked a dismal squeak as it swung, wanting to apologize for the misery it was about to unlock on us.

The bath-house was a small, dark room. After the beginning of sunrise outside, it looked wet and dismal. There was one small window high up and six wet steps that led down into the dark water. The sea came gurgling in through the lower cracks and the pale sunlight squeezing through the upper cracks striped us like zebra. I sat down on the top step because the splintery steps were more uncomfortable to my bare feet than they were to the seat of Mr. Bales' underwear.

Mrs. Bales and my sister stuck up their chins, took hands and sailed down the other five steps. When the water met their feet they screeched. Each pretended the yells were made by the other and that the noise shamed them. They gave their spare hands to each other as well as the ones that were already clasped. Then, because neither would back into the water, they sidled in together like two crabs until the sea was up to their knees. Then they began dipping alternately, clinging to each other's hands and yelling without shame. The bath-house was full to the top of shrieks. The up lady yelled and the down one gasped.

On the top step I sat shivering. I knew my turn would come and Mrs. Bales hurried it up by suddenly dropping my sister's hands, clapping her own over her mouth and screaming through her fingers, "Molars! My molars!"

Then keeping her feet stuck to the bath-house floor, she dipped her head end till only the seat of Mrs. Bales was above water with the full serge skirt swashing around it. Presently her head came up spilling sea water. She got a wet handkerchief out of her bathsuit pocket, wrapped something up in it, and rushing up the steps, laid it between Mr. Bales' boots and me. She lisped and her cheeks looked dreadfully sunken as she said, "Tramp on that, child, and it will bite!"

This reminded my sister that I was there. She tore from the water and up the stairs, seizing me with cold dead-white hands. Her arms were so strong and her hands gripped so tight I could not even kick. She dipped and dipped me. Each dip I bumped the bath-house floor. I was too full of sea to yell. When she sat me on the step again I spat water. So did my sister, so did Mrs. Bales. We spat enough water to froth the harbour. Then the ladies put on their shoes.

It was all they could do to drag themselves up the bank in their wet bath-suits. All the dust that was not laid by our drippings stuck and blackened us. On the back porch, the ladies put on dressing gowns over the tops of their wet suits, then shook and shook until the bath-suits slipped to the ground. My sister undid the boot laces that kept me inside Mr. Bales' suit. It left me suddenly.

"Mercy!" she cried and grabbed the doormat. "Here, child!" she said, "Hold that in front of you. I will walk close behind."

We hurried past the kitchen door where Sam the China boy was tapping the muffins out of their rings. The coffee smelled grand. Up the stairs we filed. You could hear all our teeth chattering.

The ladies breakfasted with bath-towels round their heads, very blue noses and dead-white fingers. Because Mr. Bales had not dipped he looked rosy, comfortable and clean. His poor underwear dripped forlornly over a barrel outside the window. It looked like Mr. Bales might have after a very bad accident. Only half of one leg! half of one arm! no apple-shaped middle and no rosy-apple head.

When we had eaten all the English muffins and honey that we possibly could, my sister and I felt better enough to start for home. We were in a hurry to brag to the others about our lovely "salt dip at sunrise."

TAR AND FEATHERS FOR SMALL

Small entered the cow barn singing. She had come to visit a young calf in the far stall. The cow was out in the pasture.

Small's singing stopped abruptly, to look for a queer noise. She decided it was coming from a platform high up and behind the cow's manger. Odds and ends were stored there, things that were not used often. There was a strong smell of tar. The workman had stowed on the platform the half bucket of tar left from tarring the back fence.

Small climbed. "You pour soul! Wait I'm coming," she gasped. She found the heaviest hen in the yard, a brahma, who wore feather trousers to her very feet, floundering in the tar bucket, hardly recognized as a hen. "For goodness sake old lady, don't splash so. I can't get near."

The hen, ambitious to find a nest above the others' nests, had fallen into the tar bucket. She was anything but the brave, begging creature that had fluttered heavily up, step by step, to seek an exalted nest. Her head was still out, but she had sealed her eyes with tar, everything except her squeaking beak; even that gurgled tar. You would never suspect that sticky black mass to be a hen.

Thinking only of the hen, Small pulled her out, and no one could picture a worse looking pair. With the hen in her arm, Small climbed down to the cow stall below. With a wisp of straw she tenderly scraped the hen.

Looking at herself, she exclaimed, "Mercy, mercy!" and ran, crying as she ran, "Mother, Mother what takes tar off?"

"Grease," said her mother without turning.

"Please give me pans and pans of grease!"

Small's mother turned. "Oh Small!"

"Mother, the brahma . . . she is tarred worse than me, you never saw such blackness. Please give me the grease. I will run and change into my worst."

"No need, child, you made a decent school-dress into your worst."

"Yes," said Small slowly, "but the hen would have died in another second. There is nothing other than her beak now, all the rest of her is tar."

Small seized the basin of fat, her mother followed. The hen was where Small had laid her, too heavy and stuck up to move.

"She had better be killed off, the creature is in a misery."

"No, no, she is our best and I love her." Since her lap could not look worse, Small sat on the straw and held the hen, greasing every feather till the stiff and tar yielded.

"What a child! I have to do the same with you when we're through with the hen," decided Small's mother.

"You are a nice mother," said Small. "Please will you get a hot bath ready for the hen, put lots of soap."

"Not one of the good wash tubs, Small!"

"No there is a rusty one. Bong used it for the cow's foot when it was bad."

The grease and the hot water and soap released the caked feathers. They dried her with soft rags and put her in the sun. Then

Mother cleaned Small's arm and hands with Old Dutch and burned the entire outfit that the child had been wearing. The hen lived, a brown tattered hen; she would never be white until after the next moult, but her stained feathers fluffed out. The smell of tar clung to Small for a week. There was black under her fingernails and grease black in her elbow creases till they wore white.

"The teacher at school says we are completely new every seven years. I suppose I have to wait seven years for it to wear off," said Small. "That is a long time. Hens manage better."

SHORT, SHORTER, SHORTEST

Father particularly liked strong durable things, be they clothes or tools or furniture or people. One day, he visited a wholesale house and home came the longest bolt of the most hideous black and white check print, enough to make dresses for all the family. Mother sighed. Her grown-up family were objecting strongly to being dressed like their little sisters. Father said that was the way to dress a family. If each had different clothes they looked like an orphanage. In those days the orphans did not wear uniforms but the Victoria population handed down all their cast-offs. We sat behind them in church and speculated much on who each garment belonged to in its pre-orphan years.

Mother cleared off the breakfast room table and got her big shears. My sister Tallie, who was pretty good at sewing, agreed to help. We were all measured. Father looked on with approval, picking up a scrap of the check and torturing it between his fingers to show how tough and strong it was. Everybody glowered according to their years and none so hard as me. I would have not only my own dress off the bolt but all the other hand-downs—as they would never wear out—when Bigger and Middle outgrew their dresses. That meant three black and white checks in graded lengths for me.

Dick was tremendously pleased that he had just gone into pants. No parent could be so cruel as to put their son into black and white cotton pants of check. Dick laughed he did not have to wear it. Father was much pleased with the effect. Bigger and Middle squirmed. The Elder and Tallie revolted and never wore their checks when we wore ours. Climb fences or trees, treat the stuff how you would, it would never wear or tear, and the black in the check was fadeless.

Now Dick and I spent most of the summer holidays with some friends at their summer camp. It was one of those delicious camps that can always be squeezed to hold one more. The boys had a bunk house built on at the end of the verandah. I shared a room with the girls my own age, one the daughter of the house and a cousin.

Our family knew no other travel luggage for small journeys than Father's carpet bag. It had violent roses crawling all over and splendidly brass fixings, culminating in an inner brass lock and a brass key almost as big as the one belonging to our front door. The two girls sat on the bed which they shared and watched me unlock and unpack the carpet bag, year after year. They knew exactly what was coming out: three black and white check dresses, sundry pinafores and my work-basket; with a long raw-cut chemise, to be made by hand in the long leisure hours in camp when someone was reading aloud.

The girls were very nicely dressed in ready made things, both dresses and chemises. But I liked sewing, and I don't think I was ever really ashamed of the checks. At least I had plenty, and my pinafores partly hid them.

There was an enormous packing case in one corner of the room with three shelves. Mine was the bottom shelf. The girls helped me unpack—at least neither of them had such a bag. Then they would say, "Here they are again, as it was in the beginning as now and ever shall be! Checks! What marvellously good wearing material your father does buy."

One day I heard my mother say to a friend, "I do love to make that child a dress out of new material. She gets all the hand downs and never complains." After that, forever, I was proud when I had three dresses of a kind at one time.

SO MUCH MORE A LADY

"Mother, need I go walking with Bigger? I am so much more a lady when I walk alone," pled Small.

"Why are you not a lady when you walk with Bigger?"

"Because she preaches all the time. 'Keep step! Take your hands out of your pockets. Keep the proper side of the road. Don't talk so loud. Don't talk at all. Don't look behind. There's not one bit of a lady about you, Small!' I'm big now, Mother, even if I am not as tall as Bigger. Let me go to town alone when you have an errand."

"You're getting big, Small, but you are young yet. You must have Bigger's company a little longer."

Off I went with Bigger. Bigger corrected and nagged. The worst trouble came on the old James Bay bridge, where the foot-walk for passengers was narrow. This provided Bigger with a grand mouthful to tell Mother when she got home.

"A man was coming towards us, a really important-looking man, Mother. He had a sports suit in loud plaid, knicker-bockers and hand-knitted stockings and a swish cane which he flourished beautifully, and he had fierce moustaches. He and Small were right in front of each other coming fast, head on. I said, 'Small, move over!' Small said, 'Shan't. He's on the wrong side, besides I'm a lady so he has to move.' He heard my order and he heard Small's answer. He gave a twirl to his cane and another to his moustache, thinking surely he'd scare the small Small, but Small did not budge. She pulled her hat right down over her eyes and would not budge an inch, and plunged into his big check middle. Oh, Mother, I was shamed, she's a dreadful child. There was a dreadful crash. The crown of Small's hat crushed flat. If he had not been so soft she could never have worn her hat again. Small stood stock still, both feet planted and grinned. The man had to go round her and to step off the sidewalk. He was furious, so furious that he 'swore'! Small polluted the family!"

Bigger said "swore'" in a whisper. It was the same as if Small swore because she provoked it.

Mother said, "I think if you did not pick at her she'd do better, Bigger. Small will lead, but she won't be pushed."

The next time Small and Bigger went out together, their Mother watched. She could see right down the street. The children went out the gate side by side and stayed together until the tall Carr poplars were passed. Then Small halted and crossed the street. In the middle, she turned and waved her hand to Bigger. Then the children walked into town abreast, but on opposite sides of the street. They came home walking the same way, and Small gave Bigger a mock bow and allowed her to go through the gate first.

COMPENSATION

Bowed down by its crop of early apples, a young tree stood in the centre of Mrs. Bales' garden. Middle and Small were visiting Mrs. Bales with their mother. While the ladies chatted, Small and Middle were sent into the garden. Hand in hand they stood looking up into the apple tree.

"If only we dared," said Small, her longing eyes on the fruit.

"That," said Middle, half a head taller than Small and two years better acquainted with the eighth commandment, "would be stealing."

Small's back was towards Mrs. Bales' house. "Middle," she said, "look over my head and see if any of Mrs. Bales' windows overlook this particular apple tree."

Middle looked. "No, they don't. Come, Small. I think we had better go down the other end of the garden." She took her sister's hand. It was better to hold onto Small. Besides, the garden was strange to the children. They did not look at the apples again, but as they turned to go, a low-hanging bough bumped their heads and two apples fell.

"Ouch!" cried Middle, rubbing her head.

"Yum!" said Small scrambling for the apples before they rolled too far.

Each child munched.

"It is not stealing when the tree throws apples at you, is it, Middle?"

"Not exactly, but even the fallen ones belong to Mrs. Bales," admitted Middle.

Small pulled the pips out of their rough little casings and ate them.

Middle nibbled close to her core but left the pips inside. Presently she scooped a hole in the earth, laid the core in it and covered it with earth.

Small nodded. "Perhaps it is safer," she said. "Mrs. Bales may have counted her apples. She wouldn't know that the tree gave them to us, would she?"

Middle said, "I was not burying the core because of that. I am expecting God to compensate Mrs. Bales by growing her a new apple tree from the pips and then she'll have ever so many more to make up for the two we ate."

"I'll do it too," said Small, beginning to dig.

Middle frowned. "I don't think God could compensate just from gristle and a tail," she said, looking at the wrecked core in Small's hand.

They went exploring till the lunch bell rang, but they were not quite comfortable inside. Lunch could easily have put apples out of their minds if it had not been that Mrs. Bales' house always smelled so strongly of ripe apples. Mother said, "What variety is that, Mrs. Bales? Their smell is delicious."

"Last year's crop," said Mrs. Bales. "I must be looking at the early tree. It ripens about now."

Small looked across at Middle, but Middle was busy manoeuvring a big mouthful and smiling up at Mrs. Bales who had just tweaked her curls. So Small looked intently at the pat of homemade butter with the acorn moulded on top and tried to keep the red from rushing to her cheeks.

After lunch Mrs. Bales drew Small into her lap resting the hollow of her cheek on Small's head. She rocked back and forth, singing a little moaning song. Small was nearly asleep when Mrs. Bales raised her head and looked across at Small's mother and said, "Couldn't you spare me this one?"

Mother shook her head. "I'm sorry, Mrs. Bales but I could not spare any of my children." She added softly, "I have known what it was to lose three."

Mrs. Bales put Small down and crossed to the sideboard. Stooping, she pulled a child's toy box from underneath. Fumbling among the trifles, some worn, some broken, she selected three tin patty pans.

"Here," she said, stuffing them into Small's pocket. "She loved these best. I used to give her dabs of my muffin batter and let her cook them in her own little tins."

The children's mother put their hats on. They started for home. Mrs. Bales stood on the verandah watching. Halfway down the path, their mother turned and went back to Mrs. Bales. She put her arm round her shoulders. The women talked while the children stood where their mother had left them.

Small said, "Middle, why do you suppose Mrs. Bales is always asking Mother to give me to her? Why do you suppose she wants me?"

"Not because you are so extra nice," said the honest Middle. "It is because Mrs. Bales had a little girl your size once and she died."

"She would not give me her little girl's things and she would not want me if she knew I was a thief, would she?"

"Certainly not."

"And she would not want me if she knew I was the sister of a thief?" Small did not wish Middle to forget that two apples fell and that Middle ate one.

Middle busied herself smelling a rose. Small squatted in the path and dug a hole in the garden bed with her fists.

"Why?" asked Middle.

"Maybe if I bury Mrs. Bales' child's patty pans, God will compensate Mrs. Bales with another little girl."

Middle frowned, "Patty pans have not got pips. I am not sure about God being able to."

"Couldn't he? Oh well, then." Small dug the patty pans up again and returned them to her pocket.

BLUE PILLS AND BLACK DRAUGHT

Those lean sallow people, strong as hay wire, make me want to bite. I was a fat rosy child, but I was subject to dreadful bilious[1] attacks. When I was sickest, my cheeks were nervous pink and my eyes bright, but oh, did I feel bad!

The remedy in those days was drastic and abominable. I hope he who invented it got his desserts. Mother knew, when you had eaten nothing all day, snarled when spoken to and drooped alone in corners, that an attack was on. She put you to bed early and you knew what was coming. Two blue pills coated with a nauseous bitter yellow powder that penetrated into every corner of your mouth no matter how quick you swallowed the pills.

After tossing all night, next morning came the Elder bearing a tumbler full of black draught,[2] which was the last straw. The Elder stood over you while you drank. She dared you to be sick and waste the draught. There was no breakfast, not that you wanted any. You only wanted to die.

1. Bilious: *connected with disturbances of the digestive process arising from too great a secretion of bile produced by the liver.*

2. Black draught: *stout or porter, a beer characterized by very deep brown colour and bitter taste.*

About five in the afternoon you crawled downstairs feeling weak as a kitten and hating everything. Invariably you found the leanest, sallowest and at the same time the most healthy family in town had come to call. They said, "Come into the garden and play."

Mother said, "Poor Small ails today."

"That child ailing!" the sallow mother would exclaim. "Why she is a picture of robustness. Look at those cheeks and that fat. She shams for the sake of being coddled. My children are never bilious."

"Come on and play," the pale freckled-faced children would tease. "Come to the cherry tree," or the plum tree, or whatever fruit was in season. They were all eating hunks of cake my mother had given them and drinking mugs of milk. The mother was a mere pale-skinned wisp of a woman. I thirsted to blue-pill and black-draft every member of the family. I hated my pink and fat.

My sisters did not understand, they never had to take blue pills and black draughts. Only Mother and Doctor Jim knew what bilious attacks felt like.

OUR CURLS

Mother's bedroom and furniture were old-fashioned but good. The drawers of the bureau kissed themselves into their slots with easy sighs. Each drawer had a lock and key of its own, and held great secrecy. The mirror was big and very just in its reflecting, neither flattering nor humbling faces. The top of the bureau was of white marble. The edges of the slab were cut in long, slow curves and bevelled. They were lovely to feel. There were little embroidered mats on the marble top and on these stood green and red bottles of Venetian glass, dainty and very fine, with slender elegant stoppers. Bay rum[1] was in one bottle and lavender water in the other. Father gave them to Mother when first they were married, "Before you children were you," Mother said. The fat pincushion was made by Bigger's careful needle stitchery and stuck with every kind of pin.

Mother stood before her bureau brushing her long dark hair. The top drawer of the bureau was open. It was partitioned into little stalls to hold mother's simple toilet things, the ones ladies used in those days to keep themselves sweet and nice. Powder was only used for babies and rouge and lipstick by the not-nice ladies, therefore it was

1. Bay rum: *a fragrant liquid originally made from the leaves of a tree growing in the West Indies, used in medicine and cosmetics.*

to be avoided. The Elder told us that much, in whispers, and left us wondering who the not-nice ladies were.

At the back of the drawer behind the brush and comb stall were three round cardboard boxes, all the boxes just alike.

"Mother, what is in those boxes?" I asked.

She opened their lids and let me see. One held baby curls nearly black—Bigger's. One, red curls very long, coiled in the round box—Middle's. One, pale short curls, nearly white—mine.

"My three little girls' first curls," said Mother, and having showed, spread the tissue paper over the top of each box with loving care and closed it.

"Why do you keep them, Mother?"

"When you have little girls of your own you will know," she smiled and smoothed my tumbled shock of brown hair back from my wondering eyes.

A few years passed and again she was before the bureau brushing her hair. She coiled her plait and pinned it and then laid away her brush and comb in their right compartment, but she did not shut the drawer. She hesitated, looking at the fire and at me. Suddenly, she slipped her hand to the back of the drawer and reached for the three boxes of curls. Hurrying as quickly as her painful breathing would allow, she crossed to the fire, dropped the three boxes on the live coals and turned quickly away.

"Mother, our curls! Mother, why are you crying?"

"Moths have got into them," she said with her back to me, looking long out of her window. "I still have my black, my red, and my little tow-head," she smiled, turning and stroking my hair.

"But my white curls have turned brown," I wailed.

TIBBY, TABBY AND TOT

You would find it difficult to suspect so stern unbendable a man as Father could be tender towards new-born kittens. It was necessary in his wholesale store for Father, to protect his goods from rats, to keep many cats. His cats were no high bred show cats. He carried bottles of milk from home to augment their rat diet.

You seldom saw any of Father's cats unless Father took you to the far end of his warehouse, where it was gloomy with piled crates that shut the light out. Father would give a little call and cats streaked out of all corners, meowing. Father knew where the mothers hid their kittens every time.

One cold mean night Father came home from town and Bigger, Middle and Small were lined up in the hall to be kissed. Instead of the usual kisses, Father said with a twinkle in his eye, "Hold out your pinafores."

Mother thought, "What have the children done now?" but we had not done anything.

Father dipped his hand three times into his great-coat pocket; each time he bought out a boneless, squirming, shut-eyed kitten.

"One for each of you," he said and looking apologetic over our heads at Mother he added, "Orphans, the mother was found drowned in the water barrel today."

Mother sighed. "We already have six cats, Richard!"

"And rats and mice, too. Could I leave these baby creatures to starve? Could I?"

Bigger's gladness was doubtful. Middle laid her kitty on her flat little chest and hugged it and soothed its mewlings.

"Kitty for my own?" squealed Small, "Oh! Oh!" and danced and hugged till the kitten yowled and Mother took it.

Mother and my big sister helped us feed the kittens till they could lap. There was much wrangling and discussions over names. Who invented the names Tibby, Tabby and Tot I do not know. Tot was Bigger's, Tabby was Middle's and Tibby was Small's. We were terribly excited when their eyes opened, more pleased than the kittens were. They squinted and blinked and were not pleased with the world at first sight. Small's kitten Tibby was an amiable creature but untidy in her habits. It did not seem possible to train her. Suddenly when half-grown she disappeared. Small was the only one who lamented or sought for Tibby. A canary bird consoled her.

Tabby and Middle were inseparable. Tabby was the lean kind. All the cats were shut into the tool-house at night otherwise they sang on the fences. One morning the cat-house door was opened and all the cats rushed out but Tabby. She was three quarters grown by then. Bong saw the tip of a ringed tabby tail sticking from under the tool chest and pulled her out. Nobody knew why she died. We gave her the most splendid funeral a cat ever had, so glorious that it even dried Middle's tears.

Little Dick's red and yellow express wagon was the hearse. Dick preceded it down the path leading to the children's gardens. In his hand was the cow bell jangling as hard as it could. Middle, as was right because she owned the corpse, dragged the wagon. Tabby was in a pink and purple shoe box, and the flowers from all the children's gardens were heaped on the bier. Mother's rag-bag was rummaged for any bits of black cloth we could find. They were tied anywhere they would tie on our persons. The most wonderful bit was a pair of black cotton gloves and a black veil. Long bitter discussion as to who should wear the veil and gloves; was it better for two mourners to wear one glove each, or should we let Middle have both, seeing she was chief mourner?

Bigger was half ashamed to take part in the funeral at all but she was the only one who had ever been to a real funeral and we relied on her to tell us how funerals were done and Bigger could not resist showing her superior knowledge. Suddenly she would have a spasm wondering if it was not sacrilegious, just over a cat. Small had to walk behind the hearse with Bigger.

"Oh, come on, Bigger! Your pinafore mourns properly. Your pinafore is splendid but I do wish you had a beard to waggle over. You can preach at the graveside." Bigger loved to preach, so she came on.

The interment was to be in Middle's garden. The soil was full of coffin boxes and very full of humps, seeing it was dug up so often for burials. All our dolls were seated on the humps leaning back against Middle's lavender and old man's beard bushes.

Tabby arrived in state and Middle tenderly stuck the box into the hole which was not deep enough and Dick was sent for the grown-up spade. It was bigger than himself; he came dragging it behind him over the gravel walk.

"Painters is looking," he announced.

Sure enough, on the lawn eating their lunch were the two painters who were painting our house. They were roaring with laughter.

Bigger looked up just as her mouth was open to begin to preach. She flung her pinafore over her head and rushed into the house. Middle stopped crying and seized the spade. Small and she piled earth on top, forgetting to deepen the grave, shovelling earth onto the box lid. They covered the glorious Tabby as speedily as possible. The dirt flew all ways, spattering the dolls.

"It was being such a splendid funeral, too!" wailed Middle.

"There, there!" comforted Small. "Painters ought to be stoned. Stop dangling that bell, Dick. It's all over."

Tot was the only orphan survivor. Bigger did not love him. He fought hard. She said he was a low sort of cat. He eluded shut-up time and went out to fight. In the morning he looked dreadful, his ears ripped and bleeding, his eyes all swollen, clotted with blood. All over his ripped coat was mud. Everyone said, "Ugh!" when they saw him and Bigger refused to own him. Tot took himself off and became a barn-cat and lived twelve years. He killed thousands of rats and Father respected him.

Small found him in the Cow Yard dead and rushed the news to Bigger.

"Your Tot is dead."

"Is he? I don't care. Don't try to revive him, Small."

"Mercy, I am glad I can never, never be your cat, Bigger! I'd rather be one of the rats Tot ate!"

KILLING THE BABY

My sister Bigger revelled in tragedy. The more awful the tragedy, the deeper her enjoyment. Not that she was cruel or unsympathetic, not by any means, but she enjoyed pulling her face as long as it would pull and toning her voice to its most mournful ring.

Bigger did not burst into the house as Middle and I did, but she always maintained a sedate rush. One day, she returned from school gasping for breath. "Oh dear!" she began, "Mother, I am sorry for that Ella who lives down the street."

"Why are you sorry for her?"

"Well, when I passed just now she was looking into the next door people's baby pram and her face was so dreadfully sad."

"Why should it be?" asked Mother.

"Well you see, that baby is the same age as her little brother, the one she killed a few weeks back. It must be awful to kill somebody!"

"I never heard that Ella killed her little brother."

"Didn't you? Well, her mother told the other children they were not to tell, but they did, and it got all over the school."

"How did it happen?"

Bigger always sprinkled "well" through her conversation, particularly if the situation she described was not well. "Well," a long pause while she stretched her naturally long features longer and we all stood agape. "You see, Ella was minding the baby and rounding up the cows at the same time, out there on the pasture land above the Dallas Road cliffs. Ella shooed a bad cow with the pram. The front wheels went a mite too far, slipped over the edge and the handle slid out of Ella's hand. The pram rolled down the bank and overturned. The baby spilled out and he struck his head on a stone."

"Oh," said Mother, "Poor little Ella, and the poor mother trying to shield her little girl and mourning her dead baby at the same time. Bigger, you must not repeat this story!"

"All right Mother, I won't, though . . . it is rather nice to have something to tell that makes people's eyes pop and their voices hush."

The harrowing story about the killed baby impressed me deeply. Shortly after I heard this conversation, I went to visit my married sister. Her first baby was a couple of months old. It was the first baby in the family. Everybody made an absurd fuss over it. Bigger, Middle and I were enthusiastic over being aunts and my little brother, on being told that he was the only uncle of the infant, howled and begged to be allowed to be an aunt like the girls.

While I was spending the day my married sister said, "I want some groceries. Will you go down the street and get them for me?" She added, as if conferring a great favour on me, "You may take baby in her pram, the air will be good for her." It was the first time I had been trusted out alone with the baby. She gave me minute instructions about locking the wheels when the pram stood still.

Mr. Fell's fine grocery store was only a few blocks away. It had a big show-window and was on Fort street. The door straddled across the corner. From his store door Mr. Fell could look down three streets at once. The sidewalk had a very elegant tilt up to the entrance of the store. Victoria had not plumbed herself yet. Open surface gutters ran down the sides of each street. Clear water trickled in them and grass grew very green at every gutter's side. The sidewalks were wooden and wide and Mr. Fell's corner was sidewalked especially fancy. The planks spread fanwise, a sunburst effect from the door to the street.

I felt very grown up with Mr. Fell calling out "Miss" and a pram to push. I spread the shopping list on the counter and Mr. Fell went through it with me. I asked, "Are the eggs fresh? Are the apples sound?" I doubled up my pinafore to carry the little parcels in it to the pram and Mr. Fell took the heavy ones. I said, "I have the pram waiting," with as grand an air as children now-a-days say, "The motor is waiting."

But when we got to the door we stood aghast. The pram was gone! I remembered I had forgotten to lock the wheels. The dreadful story of Ella's pram that ran away came vividly before me.

"Mr. Fell," I whispered, "I've killed my sister's baby, perhaps." I did not scream or even cry. I just lived the tragedy, with me for Ella. Mr. Fell put an arm round me to keep me from falling.

"Come, come, little lady, no harm is done." He pointed to the runaway pram sitting in the ditch with the baby peacefully sleeping inside. He hauled it back onto the sidewalk, packed the groceries around the baby, went into the store again and came out with a huge chocolate for me. "The youngster ain't hurt a mite. Don't look so white about it, little 'un."

While my sister unpacked the groceries, I never took my eyes off the baby. My sister, having emptied the pram of all but the baby, locked the wheels and left her in the garden to finish her nap.

"Oughtn't she to wake?" I could not keep my voice quite steady.

"Oh no, she is far too wakeful."

Suppose she never woke! Suppose when she woke her eyes were imbecile from the bump!

"You must start for home now. Mother will be wondering," my sister said.

"Let me stay till the baby wakes," I pleaded.

But the baby slept on.

"Come," said my sister, "it is getting dusk."

She went into the next room and I gave the child a poke which made her squirm. Then I gave a pinch that made her yell. Satisfied, I set off home.

I said to Bigger, "How long did it take that baby to die after he bumped his head?"

"Oh, I don't know," she said shortly. "Don't you be crazy enough to go and ask Ella. Mother said not to mention it to anyone."

"But I have a special reason."

They marvelled at the extraordinary devotion I showed my young niece for the next few weeks, always asking one or another of the grown ups, "Do you think the baby is quite healthy?" I got the family jittery by continually inquiring, "She is quite normal isn't she?"

My mind was made up, as soon as any queer symptoms developed, I would go to the police and give myself up. I would spare Mother that. Mr. Fell was an alderman or something very important, besides being an honourable man. He would have to tell the truth and was the only witness. I would go straight to the police office close by the high board jail fence with broken glass on top. I would say to the policeman in charge, "I have killed my sister's baby. How soon do you want to hang me?" I saw my black stockinged legs, my serge dress and white apron, my undies scandalously visible because of hanging so high above the jail wall. I saw the headline in the Colonist: "Youthful Murderess Kills Sister's Child."

The baby who had always been a poor sleeper suddenly began sleeping well, almost all day as well as all night. Terror seized me. The rest of the family were thankful of the sleep. I read somewhere about someone who went into a coma and then died. Could one be coming on? At last I could bear it no longer. I went to Mother.

"Come," she said and opened her arms. "Tell me all about it."

She had seen by my condition something was worrying me terribly.

"Poor little girl," she said, "Poor little girl. You have suffered cruelly, just because you forgot to lock the wheels. Remember next time. And now—forget all about it. My little granddaughter is in perfect health."

THE FAMILY PLOT

The old Quadra Street Cemetery was a lovesome place, but now it was as full as the law would allow. So they put a chain and padlock round the pickets of the gate to keep the dead in and the living out, and dedicated a new portion of cleared raw ground at Ross Bay for Victoria's burying. It was a treeless, wind-swept place, of gravely soil and blaring sunshine. One side of the "New Cemetery" was bounded by the sea. It was raised above it by a medium-high rough grassy bank. The other side was bounded by the highway, over which ran periodically a noisy rural tram line.

Like all public projects, there was a good deal of wrangling over the changed location. The whole town, Small's father and his family included, went out to inspect the New Cemetery. One person thought this, and one that, about it. It was so different from the old cozy, near-in cemetery that was so easy of access. However, we supposed we had to grow, and cemeteries could not go on expanding in the middle of cities. We might as well swallow Ross Bay as a burying ground and stop fussing.

But how different they were! The hard cold gravestones of the old place were gentled by the vines and brambles that tied them together in friendly fashion. The tall trees round the border, that had leaves with silvery white backs, dappled the overgrown greenery of the graves with shadow.

At first the old-timers cried out at carrying their dead to the bare new lonesome place. The graves looked so sparse and desolate with the great empty spaces between. No hugging brambles, no twining honeysuckle, everything bleak and raw, new and rough, nothing to tie grave to grave chummily. The dry grass parched quickly under the glaring sun, perpetual wind off the sea rattled and creaked among it up on the ridge.

To be eligible to lie in the Old Cemetery, you only had to be dead, there was no sorting of race and creed. In the new it was different. The High and Low Church did not mix, nor could the Roman Catholics, Jews, Presbyterians and Atheists lie beside each other; they each had a different part allotted to them.

In 1886, Small's mother died. It was the first time that a death in the house had been experienced by the younger members of the family. Stillness fell on their home, their garden, on the whole world it seemed. In the house, the hush centred in the drawing room where Small's mother lay in her coffin, at peace after her long, long suffering. Serenely indifferent to the hurt that was all about her. She who had been so sympathetic to the smallest suffering of any of her family.

Father sat in the old "praying chair" in the sitting room all day, not only for family worship. He was broken, silent, not even ashamed of the tears that would run down, hurrying to hide in his beard. His eyes stared but they looked at nothing.

Upstairs the family and some neighbours who had come to help were sewing black. On the bed lay a huge roll of silk crepe. It had cost a lot of money, that crepe, but there were five women to be clothed in mourning, besides the armlets on Fathers and Dick's coats and on all our overcoats. We wanted to show Mother every atom of respect we could, and in 1886 that was one of the ways to do it.

Small was not much help in the sewing room upstairs. For the moment, the nearly-blind old lady who insisted on coming to trim our hats was supplied with a pincushion full of threaded needles, and all the basting threads were pulled out of the sewing till some more were put in. Small was appointed "Odd Jobs," one of which was to look in on Father very often and see that he wanted nothing. Small was afraid to speak. She just passed through the room, in at one door, out at the other.

He called, "Small!"

"Yes, Father."

"Tell your sisters I wish to speak to them, Small."

"Very well, Father."

They circled round his chair.

"I have called you," Small's father said, "to discuss with you the choosing of the family burial plot. It is a question that concerns us all. We shall all lie there eventually, myself beside your Mother before long. 'Three-score years and ten', that is God's allotted age for Man."

Father always maintained that statement, and kept up to time two years later. Small held that Father would have thought it equivalent of giving God "back chat" not to have died at the age of three-score and ten years.

It was the first time Father had allowed his children to have a voice in family affairs. Bigger and Middle's minds had not been considered adult enough; as for Small! she was not sure now whether she was to have a voice or not.

Her father looked at his two eldest daughters who shook their heads then he looked at Bigger and Middle.

Bigger said, "You choose, Father." And Middle said nothing.

Small stepped a little closer to the praying chair hoping to remind her father she was there. He was reminded of Small.

"And you?" he said, seeing her eagerness.

"I chose the spot I wanted the first time we went to see the New Cemetery, Father."

"That was strange. Why?"

"I just liked it, not much, but better than the rest."

"Why did you like it?"

"It seemed to me the only comfortable spot in all the cold bleakness. It has two willow trees growing on it, the only trees in the whole New Cemetery. It lies in a little hollow right in the centre of Ross Bay's curve. The sea gulls swoop in from one end of Ross Bay, circle the two willows and circle out again, carrying their cries out to sea."

Father frowned. "I do not like that low-lying dip, Small. It is damp, unhealthy."

"Do dead people mind damp?"

The Elder said, "Trees on graves are not good."

"Why?"

"Their roots creep about and pierce into the seams of coffins. It is a horrible idea."

"I think it would be splendid to be useful to the earth after you were no more use to yourself, splendid to feed a tree!" said Small.

The Elder was all ready with a tongue click of disgust when Father closed the conversation by saying, "Here is the undertaker. Get your hats on." He nodded to Small, "You are to come as well as your oldest sister." Small felt important, almost grown up.

The Elder's face was unpleasant when she saw the two scrawny, hungry-looking little willows. Father frowned at the comparative nearness of the willows to the bank. He said, "They've talked long about that retaining wall; dear knows when they will build it. Meantime high tide breakers are dashing against the bank. That's bad."

The undertaker came from the cemetery lodge. He had a plan of the cemetery plots in his hands. "This way, sir. The better class plots are up on the ridge."

Father did not care a bit about style but he wanted the best there was for Mother. High, dry, healthy. He bought on the ridge. He leant a little heavily on Small's shoulder as he climbed the slight incline as though he felt the weight of his three score years and ten. He saw Small turn for a last look at the two willow trees, after his decision was made. "Small, you got your love of trees from me." He smiled down on the little girl, feeling her disappointment.

Someone else bought the plot with the willows. The willows thrived and grew sturdy and beautiful. Small always felt a little cheated when from the ridge she looked into the hollow and saw the willows.

Up on the ridge the wind always blew and the sun always scorched and brittled the grass between the graves. A streetcar rattled by every twenty minutes. The sea gulls never troubled to come that far inland to cry for the dead, nor were there any drooping willow boughs to sweep across the graves. Small used to wonder if the dead felt any healthier up there than down in the hollow.

BEAUTIFUL EYES

I now wonder how I came to miss their blue beauty the first sixteen years of my life. I had to have it shown to me through hearing a chance conversation between my father and my big sister.

It was soon after Mother's death and it was my father talking. It was Dick he was talking about. Dick, the son he despised for being sickly. "Curious chap. He ought to have been the girl and this one," he pointed to me, "the boy."

"Why curious?" asked the Elder. To her way of thinking we youngsters were all curious. Because of Mother's delicacy, the Elder had bossed us for many years. As a mother she was not a success, not having mother-ways. "In what way do you find the boy curious, Father?"

"I was hilling my potatoes and paused to rest at a hill. I stepped aside to examine the alfalfa hay just cocked. The boy was on the far side of the cock, thrown back against it. His arms were behind his head, his eyes staring straight up into the sky. So busy with his dreams was he that he neither saw nor heard me. I did not speak. I left him to his dreams, to his sky-staring."

My sister said, I did not know her voice could go so soft, "Dick has the most beautiful eyes I have ever seen."

Father grunted.

I ran from the room. I knew where to find Dick and I wanted to see this beauty of his eyes for myself. Dick was in the Cow Yard building a house out of old pickets that had been ripped off a fence, to be replaced by new. It was a crazy-looking structure he was building, but it must have been put together strongly, for it stood many, many years in the Cow Yard, always known as "Dick's Castle."

"Dick, when will it be finished?" I asked.

Dick looked at me straight. The Elder was right. Yes, blue, blue with long black lashes and level black brows. Eyes that could twinkle as well as dream.

"Did you know, Father says in a few years I can go East to college and by and by I can study to be a doctor?"

"Oh, a doctor! Will your house have a door and a window and a doctor's plate in brass?"

"I have not thought that far yet."

"You might paint one to put in the window."

"Perhaps, a house that does not have to be shut up would be nicer."

I wondered what Dick had been dreaming about on the hay cock. What castle in the air had he been building? Was it his surgery?

Dick's eyes were beautiful. They were exactly like Father's must have been before his turned adult, changed from boy's blue to man's steel grey, and his eyebrows levelled and overhung them. Father's eyes still had the same twinkle as Dick's, only he doused the twinkle out most of the time.

Perhaps Father's eyes had been boyishly dreamy too, once. Perhaps this home of ours in the New World was one of Father's boy-dreams. Perhaps the dream we were living in right now once had no door or window. Perhaps when he saw the dreaming in Dick's eyes he softened, remembering his own, listened and melted when his son wanted to go away and study to be a doctor.

AUNTIE

In our dislike of each other, Aunt and I were evenly matched, only she hypocritted, veiling her dislike under innumerable "dears," while I made no secret of my feelings towards Aunt. She was only a mock Aunt anyhow. She and Mother came out from England as brides, in a sailing ship all round the Horn. As it took six months, they had ample time to get to know each other. Mother said she was a nice, sweet girl till her husband babied and spoilt her and made her hideously selfish. That was how we children knew her, selfish.

After thoroughly spoiling her, her husband died, and she came rushing up to Victoria to cry on Mother's shoulder. It was the first time we younger children had seen Auntie. Mother met the boat. We children were clustered round the front gate, waiting. She was fat and pompous, not gently dignified like Mother. I knew straight away I did not like her. She stepped from the cab and handed Mother all her hand-luggage, then she sailed through the gate.

"Kiss Auntie," she said and looked us over. "Emily, my satchel! I would not dare pass that lily without protection."

She pointed to Father's *Lillium Auratum*[1] magnificent with its

1. Lillium Auratum: *common name Gold-Band Lily. Blooms Aug. or early Sept. on 4-6 ft. plants. Flowers are fragrant, waxy white and spotted crimson.*

fifty blooms. First she anointed her nose from a fancy bottle, then she stuffed a handkerchief up to each nostril and strode past the lily. The whole month of her visit she hinted and hinted to Father that it would oblige her if he uprooted the thing. It was beneath her window and perfumed the whole garden. Strong scented flowers gave her rose-cold.[1]

Father said, "Quite unfortunate, you will have to pick another month for your visits in future." And his lovely lily bloomed on.

She made us wait on her hand and foot. I wished she would say to me, "I hate you!" instead of kissing me and "dear"ing me; saying over and over, "Auntie wishes this," and "Auntie wishes that." I hated saying "Aunt" when she was not aunt to us by rights.

She cried for Uncle whenever she remembered. He had left her very well off. She felt herself a very desirable widow, particularly when a certain "Mr. Hawkins" called. Then she came rustling into the room in crepe and black silk, with her eyes all a-twinkle and lips smiling.

When Aunt cried it began with an explosion, just like a blown up paper suddenly popped. She battled her bursting way out of the room blindly, overturning everything but the piano and sofa.

On Sunday evenings we sang hymns. The Elder played and we all stood round the piano and chose a hymn in turn. While Aunt was with us I always chose, "Go Bury Thy Sorrow." Father, Mother and Aunt stayed listening in the sitting room with the doors open so they could hear. One verse of "Go Bury" was enough. We heard the bursting explosion above even the Elder's pounding and our roaring and then we heard the rustle of silk sweeping up the stairs, and a fresh burst every third step.

1. *hay fever*

She had just performed one night when the doorbell rang. She leaned over the bannister and when she had washed her eyes she rustled down the stairs in no time, starry-eyed and cheerful, to meet Mr. Hawkins. Ordinarily it took "Hold the Fort" double loud followed by the clatter of tea cups to bring her down after a "burst."

Mr. Hawkins did not marry Aunt. He never got any further than bringing her stale "Birmingham papers" and one box of sweets which she complained were inferior to San Francisco sweets.

Aunt went back to California and married a widower. He was French and had three half-grown children. Being her stepchild must have been worse than being her mock-niece.

Aunt bought the love of the rest of the family with five dollar gold pieces. Her purse was stuffed with them. It did not mean more to her to give a five than giving away ten cents meant to most people. My married sister went to visit in San Jose once. When she was coming home Aunt opened her purse and laid a five dollar gold piece on the table for each member of the family. She skipped me.

My sister picked up the gold, naming the child it was for, "Bigger, Middle, Small."

"Stop! not Small—Dick!"

"And Small?" asked my sister.

"Small? Oh, you can take these to Small." She opened a drawer and pulled out a shabby pair of black kid gloves.

"I have only worn them a few times," she said.

Aunt's hands were enormous. When my sister gave them to me, I ripped the kid clean across the palm of each glove and threw them on the floor and stamped on them.

"I don't want her old gloves, or her dirty gold," I said. "Tell her—tell her how I appreciated her generous gift!"

"You are not going to write Auntie and thank her?"

"I am not!"

It was not till I went to the San Francisco Art School that I tasted the full flavour of Aunt. It was ordered by the powers that ruled our home, that I should spend the long summer vacation in San Jose with Aunt. I rebelled. It was no good. I was only allowed my school fees and my board during the school term, so there was nothing for holidays. I had to go.

I led the stepdaughters into pranks, hoping it would put Aunt off inviting me next time, but it never worked. She felt it a duty to my dead mother, whom Aunt really had loved. The girls liked to have me, but the edge was blunted off the fun by Aunt's everlasting bullying.

The first two weeks of my stay she spent correcting the bad habits I had acquired since I last visited her; the next four she spent preparing me for the term to come. She told all her friends and ours I was a very bad girl and that I was the only Carr that ever sassed her Auntie. That Auntie title was rubbed in like goose grease on a wheezy chest, and I boiled!

Aunt's spare room was at the end of a long black corridor, quite isolated from the rest of the upstairs. Aunt and husband slept downstairs, the two stepdaughters in the room directly above theirs. I had always been a baby about the dark. The spare room was very big. I begged that one of the girls be allowed to sleep with me in the enormous bed. Aunt refused. I used to stay awake half the night shaking.

One night I crept out of the bed and raised the blind, perhaps old moon would shine in and help me bear the dark. Zip! up flew the blind with a whiz, the moment I touched the cord. There looking in at me were two globes of fire. They were eyes, I knew. I dashed out the door and down the corridor.

"Oh girls, there are eyes looking in my window! I can't go back. Let me in, your beds are wide. Oh, one of you let me share!"

The biggest girl got out of bed and went to my room.

"It's a cat, booby," she said, "Go on back." But I could not.

"Momma will hear—and then!"

"I don't care if she does!"

Each got into her own bed and drew the bed clothes over her head. They put the light out and were quiet.

Stealthily I pushed one bed up to the other. The castors rolled quiet and easy. Before the beds touched I pulled up the hang-over bed clothes; then I climbed over the foot, lay down in the crack and pulled the edges of their blankets over me. It was not comfortable. I was nearly asleep and thought they were when a stealthy foot slipped out and kicked the other bed. The two beds rolled apart. I fell to the floor with a thud. Everybody laughed but me, and then the girls did go to sleep. I got up and went to their piles of neatly folded clothes. I slithered the beds together again and tied them leg to leg with the girls' stockings, the near leg of one bed to the near leg of the other.

In the morning Aunt sent for the three of us. She was propped in bed behind an enormous tray of breakfast.

"What was that thud I heard above me last night?"

"It was me falling out of bed. I slept in the crack and they pushed the beds apart."

"Why did you leave your own room?"

"Because I can't and I won't sleep there alone. It's a beastly room."

We looked each other full in the eyes. Aunt's dropped first.

To the youngest stepdaughter she said, "You have to sleep with that baby in the spare room, I suppose."

Her cheeks pinked at being beaten. She wanted peace for her own self.

"Yes, Momma."

"Thanks." I would not say "Auntie."

CORSETS

It was not considered decent for girls in their teens, particularly fat girls, to go corsetless. My round body rebelled violently at the restriction. Middle and Bigger, the sisters two and four years older than I, were lucky in being stock size. Mother knew just what to ask for in the shops for them. There were few things that she had to make at home for them. Nothing ever fitted me. She had to make every stitch I wore.

My sisters felt elegant when they slipped from the corded stays of childhood to boned corsets. How glad I would have been to slide my body back into the soft clothes of early girlhood. My breadths were always too wide for my lengths. The buttons always burst off my dresses and petticoats. If my angry muscles could not expand, what else could the buttons do?

Corsets are an invention of the devil. These cruel metal hooks that fasten the front, those unforgivable steels that cut into your ribs and finally break and prick groans out of you. The nasty little bits of whalebone like a miniature picket fence running round the skin of your stomach, then "doing up" and "undoing," what agony. The lowest clip must be done up first, then the highest and the lowest must be undone again, while the three middle hooks give vicious pinches at your skin as each is hooked. Sometimes the performance must be done several times before your organs were properly hugged into the corset for the day. The corset brutes were hot, too. The material was stout and practically made double, too, because of the bone casings.

There was no escape. You had to wear corsets and it was much hardest on the fat girls. The corsets laced up the back, and it was possible for an Elder to see how sloppy you looked and pull them in for you. They were always got for you several sizes too small, to allow pulling in of a grown-up. You could not fix the strings behind your back without snarls and knots.

Corsets had one good use. They kept your stockings taut. On the other hand, they told if you left them off even if you concealed under a loose coat. They let out on you by tumbling your stockings round your ankles. Corsets were a curse.

At the age of twelve I pondered, "Was a corsetted life worth living?" Mother pointed to a couple of uncorsetted women who had let their figures ramble. One woman was lean, one fat; they were both unforgivably hideous. They came to a picnic with us once and, when they bent over the tablecloth spread upon the grass to reach the food, they did look awful.

Mother had to take some pretty strong measures to get me inured to corsets. I did the worst I could with my first pair. It was appalling how soon they wore out. Coming into my bedroom one night, Mother was horrified at the wreckage of whalebone and steel round my waist.

"I must get you a new pair, child."

"Oh, Mother, don't please. These have only got half used to me!"

She had no mercy. The new ones were bought.

"It is nearly my birthday," I begged. "Can't I wear the old ones till after that?"

Coming home from school, I passed a little corner store selling everything. In the window were some corset bones, just raw steel, no covering. I bought some new fronts and some new side steels and went home and slaved all evening. I covered the bones with stout calico from Mother's piece bag. Next day hurrying from school I went to my room and sewed again till bedtime on my corsets. Half of what I know about sewing (and I am a good sewer) was learned on that old pair of corsets. When I took the mended corsets to Mother, she was amazed at my performance, and for a treat let me wear them a little longer.

I knew time was nearly up. It neared the date of Mother's semi-annual visit to town to outfit us for winter. A hired hack came. The three little girls, Bigger, Middle and Small, the young brother and Mother got in, picturing the shoes, the hats, the coats we were going to have. One corner of my happiness was blighted. I just knew I'd be taken to the lady in the corner of Mr. Wilson's dry goods store behind bolts of cloth and be corsetted. The lady was perfectly straight up and down herself. She might as well have been pushed into a drainpipe.

She looked at me critically and said, "We only keep stock sizes. People just have to take the nearest to their age and take in or let out." They were black sateen embroidered with yellow silk and too abominable for imagining. The straight up and down lady said the silken laces and all were far too handsome for a girl my age but she had another in stock with less lace.

I got through one aching week. I even cried at the misery under my desk at school.

Middle and Bigger were doing their home lessons. The Elder and Mother were out.

"You answer the door bell, Small."

It was the little foolish person who lived near us.

"Your mother in, child?"

"No, Mother is out."

"It is important," she said, then, "He, he, he," she began to laugh. It was a way she had, poor thing, she was not quite right in the head. "Counting you there are five women in this house," she said. "I thought someone might have an extra pair they could lend for a week. If he gets them today he says, they can be back in a week. He, he, he. I'd be dreadfully obliged if I could borrow . . . while mine are renovate?"

"What is it you want to borrow?"

"A corset."

"I have a brand new pair you can have and welcome. No hurry about returning."

"He, he," she giggled, "You! I never thought of you. I'm dreadfully lean. You? You're fat."

"They'll lace tight. Wait!"

I flew upstairs to my room and came back with the black and gold corset warm from my body.

"He, he, he," the poor weak wit said, and tucked them under her arm and hurried away.

It was a very hot afternoon but when Mother came home I was going around in a great coat with the perspiration running down my face. Mother touched my hot face and remarked there was no measles about.

"I'm not measled, Mother."

Mother looked suspiciously down at my ankles. My stockings hung in wrinkles. She laid a hand against my ribs and sighed. "Where are they?"

"Lent."

"Your new corset? But to whom?"

"The 'he, he' woman. Poor creature, she came in such distress. She had one pair and they had to go to be renovated. She said as there were five women in our house, she thought we could spare a pair, only on loan, you know."

"How much money have you in your penny bank?"

"That won't half buy a corset. I will lend you the balance till you are caught up again. Mrs. 'he, he' can keep yours. Perhaps it will teach you not to lend your clothing. Lending your underwear! Ugh! I never!"

KISSING

She was old teen age, I was young teen age, when we discussed kissing. We both came of very English families who believed in orgies of kissing preceding and following every family event.

"I have heard it stated," said Elsie, "That it is a very unhealthy, unwholesome habit, this kissing."

"It must be," I said with a little girl's admiration of a big girl's superior knowledge. "Especially where there are beards," I added. "And I must say, when there is a beard it is ticklish and horrid, especially on foggy evenings, no matter how you love. What about giving it up, all except tremendous occasions? Fathers, mothers and maybe the whole family on Christmas or birthdays might be excepted? Otherwise, no kissing."

My friend was fifteen and had a lot to learn yet. I was eleven and had a great deal more to learn than my friend.

"Of course I'd have to kiss Papa," Elsie said doubtfully, "even if he has got a beard, because he is a clergyman and expects it."

"We except him," I allowed graciously, "but mind you, Elsie, aunts, cousins, friends we don't know much, have got to leave our cheeks alone. Because they are round and pink they think they have a right to kiss them. What right have strangers to dart at little girls, yum, yum, as if they were preachers? I wish I'd have been a boy. Well, good-bye," I jumped the ditch and waved my hand. "Remember, Elsie, when we meet, if I just bow and say 'Hello', I'm not mad at you."

New Year's Day was the first real test. I don't know how Elsie managed, but I know I did not get half a chance to be firm. In those days, all the gentlemen friends of the family called to wish Mother and her family the "compliments of the season." Of course none of them ever kissed Mother, but they took it out on Mother's children. The older the men were, the more they kissed, and the old ones all had beards. It was no good to try to back, they followed till you were up to the wall. Then it was a hard kiss with no spring, only a hard wall-bump so firmly planted that the kiss was almost cruel.

Elsie kept her pact with me, but a few years later she married. I never saw her do it, but she was a very fond sweetheart and I am absolutely certain she broke the pact many months before she married. I expect she was glad I was in San Francisco or somewhere when they were engaged and married, so that I did not have to see her kiss him at the altar.

Kissing dogs, cats, birds was a different matter; the creatures were never embarrassed nor made you embarrassed. Apart from the genuine love you had for them, it was a convenient let-off to loving and you just had to love.

My third sister was ultra-kissy. When, after my pact with Elsie, she saw me squirming to get out of being kissed, she said, "You are unloving and wicked. Bye and bye you will kill peoples' love for you."

That made me stop and think for a moment! I did not want to kill love. But she made a duty of kissing. If you were going away, or it was bedtime, she'd kiss you. If there were strangers there to see, she'd kiss you extra hard, because she wanted everyone to know what a devoted family we were. It was correct in old-fashioned English families to be devoted, to exhibit profuse kissing.

I was really fond of that excessively kissy sister. There was so much in her to admire. But, as I told her once, I loved her much the best if there was an ocean or a continent between us. Or perhaps I should have said, out of kissing reach. If she'd been honest, she'd have said the same. There was so much in me of which she disapproved, it falsed out our kisses.

Middle, the sister next to me, was not the same. She was undemonstrative and indifferent. We were always pals and shared things. I never dodged her kisses. They were lukewarm, businesslike affairs. We shared a room. It was always our custom on going to bed to blow out the candle, sit up in the dark, each push a hand under our pillow and pull out a fine rosy apple put there in the morning when we made our beds. Munch, munch, in the sharp cold dark. My sister put her apple core into the candlestick-tray. I flung mine under the bed and had seven scoldings every Saturday morning when the room was cleaned. We kissed and lay down after the apple-eating. Middle was very aware of my shortcomings, but she thought they were my own business. Bigger shouldered the wickedness of the entire world and thought a kiss fixed everything.

So, in young girlhood I kissed my Mother for the joy and comfort of it, the next three sisters I kissed for duty, Middle I kissed because it was natural to do so and I loved her very deeply, and my brother I kissed Sunday nights. This habit came about because my brother and I went to stay every summer with some friends at the seashore. The mother, very English, tried to insist on family goodnight kissing, every day, but the boys refused to kiss more than once a week. Dick and I thought the plan rational, so on returning home followed suit and kept it up.

Elsie raised a large family, and of course when she became a wife and a mother her habits changed, so in a general way the pact was off. We have been very dear friends all our life, but to this day when we meet we do not kiss, we clasp each other's hands, smile and remember.

After our family was reduced to two and that two was Middle and me, everything was so sad and lonesome that automatically we began to kiss again. But soon it dawned on me that Middle did not care much about kissing, either. She stuck out her jaw bone and I picked. If she kissed anything it was the air.

"Let's quit this jawbone kissing, it doesn't mean anything," I said.

"All right," she answered, so promptly I think she was glad. By and by one of us nearly died and Middle of her own free will began to kiss me again. Well, so much for family and promiscuous kissing. I often wonder, do angels kiss?

There are other kisses that do count, count tremendously, and they are not necessarily given and taken by blood relatives. Your heart does it and the lips don't count and you cannot lay any laws down about it because it would not obey. It has no excuse, no shame, and there it is something beautiful about kissing, and it is no good trying to dodge. But these are adult kisses, a man's to a woman and a woman's to a man. They are different. They are from the heart. Elsie and I did not discuss this kind, at that immature age we could not.

CHIVALRY

My brother was four years younger than I. Between us we got all the whippings in our family. For myself they made me mad, but I knew some were deserved. But to know that wicked little whip was curling round Dick's lanky stockinged calves, to hear the scuffle and the swish, turned me sick. He was so lean and so weak.

One morning a bad one was going on. The door was shut but I could hear and I turned deadly sick and leaned against the verandah post. A neighbour on his way to town saw my face from the gate as he passed. He ran up the garden path.

"Little girl, what is the matter? You are white as a ghost!"

I pointed to the door, he could hear for himself. He turned away and sneaked off to town. He and his wife were some of my sister's "remittance protégés." She spoiled and pampered his neurotic and complaining wife. Not for anything would he anger my sister by interference, no matter who was being beaten.

While he stood there my sister's angry voice shouted, "Serves you right, if you had not writhed, the whip would not have cut your ear!"

Dick came from the room, paler by contrast with the trickle of red blood that ran down his cheek from the cut on his ear.

Fury seized me. "Do what I did, she never whips me now, not since I said, 'No' after the big one. You remember, when the Bully (another remittance man) complained that I had insulted him by saying he was no gentleman. Well, when I was on my feet again I said, 'That is the last! I am fifteen now. The next time you beat me I hit back.' She has never struck me again, before that I got one or more every day. Try it, Dick."

Dick looked at me out of those clear, glorious blue eyes in their dark settings. "Thanks, old girl," he said. "But you see, it's different, I'm not yet eleven. You were fifteen and . . . That's not the reason . . . She's a woman . . . I'm, a man." He blushed boyishly, looking so young. "At least I shall be some day. Men can't hit women, see?"

Shortly after that Dick was sent to boarding school in the East. He never lived at home again. Later he contracted T.B. and was advised to move to southern California to live. He died there at the age of twenty-eight. He made many, many friends. They wrote to us at his death, calling him by their own special endearment name, and with that name invariably they coupled two words, "gentle and chivalrous."

A THREE-GIRL DRAWING CLASS

I was the youngest of the three girls who composed the little class, youngest by a couple of years. A young woman, an artist, started this drawing class in the old Rocabella boarding house. We three attended and I got little attention. The other two had money; that is, one did in her own right, the other had a rich uncle behind her.

I was a dead-head in the class. I earned my tuition by lending the teacher my collection of plaster casts, as she could find none in Victoria. Having heard that was the way they taught in Art Schools, I had saved up my pocket money and sent away for quite a good collection and had also cast pieces of my friends and myself. It was difficult to teach oneself without guidance. When the lady advertised for plaster casts, I went to her and offered her my casts in return for lessons. I was helpful and it was an ordeal but the lady was glad to get my casts.

The teacher was pretty and had a beau to whom she preferred serving tea in her studio than teaching girls to draw. Our lessons ended very promptly when the young man came to tea. He kissed her just as if we'd been three chairs and had no blushes.

The wealthy girl's term was very brief in the Rocabella class, then off she went to England to study. She was to stay at Alexandra

House, a swell home for students, and to attend Westminster School of Art. That was all right, she had money—let her. The other girl and I worked on happily enough, till one day she burst into the studio too full of news to be articulate. "My rich English uncle is going to put me through art school. He is paying my fare, paying my keep at Alexandra House, paying my fees at Westminster School of Art!"

Bitter jealousy foamed in my heart. I had not an uncle in the world, leave alone a rich one. I had only a mock aunt who had lots of money but hated me because I "sassed" her.

"When do you go?" I asked with a bitter shaking voice which I could not quite control.

"Right away. You'll be here all alone. Then I expect teacher's beau won't think you are worthwhile minding, you work so hard, and he will spend all lesson time here."

Tears of self-pity fell down among the charcoal sharpenings and rubbing-out bread in my lap. I could not help mourning over my sorry lot a little, but I worked on alone and learned a certain amount, not so much from the teacher as from the steady weekly application. No more pupils came. The teacher thought it not worthwhile to rent a room in which to teach the one dead-head pupil, so she went away and there was no more class.

By and by my Guardian (my parents being dead) permitted me to go to San Francisco and attend the Mark Hopkins School of Art. It was not London, but I learnt a lot and now I am glad I made my start here in the West rather than in London. I studied in San Francisco for three and a half years, then I went home and taught children to draw.

I made a studio out of an old hayloft over the cow's stall in the barn. Children liked coming to the studio because it was funny and I had creatures so close. I was happy teaching there, but still in the back of my mind was a greed for more, more, more understanding of the thing I loved best in the world, painting. So I said to myself, "I'll do it too! I'll do it by myself" and I started to save. I had lots of pupils and when they paid my very modest fees, I hoarded the money in an old pair of boots hanging from the rafters in the barn studio. My father's estate kept me, so that I had no living expenses.

At last I said, "Thank you old shoes, I always rather believed in your luck, though my sisters do think it superstitious and they consider superstition at war with religion." I emptied the shoes and took the money out and bought a ticket. I arranged the rest in the bank so that I could get it in England, then I went.

Of course the other two girls from Victoria were miles ahead of me now. They had both had things hung in the Royal Academy. One girl had left Westminster; she had married and I think was travelling. The other one, the one with the uncle, was there still. She was a link with home, but a little uppish because she had so long a start ahead, and the rich uncle still supported her and her art. She was strong in cities, while city life was always making me ill. I had rotten health which delayed me too. Of course I could not afford to live in Alexandra House where she lived. I had a cheap boarding house.

I never tried for the Academy; it was not my ambition. Besides, you had to frame in real gold leaf and there were other expenses connected, and then of course after all the expense you might be rejected. English people's opinion of Colonials, as they called us in those days, was very poor. When I went to see the Academy show, it was not the kind of painting I wanted to learn. It did not fit Canada. I was sorry I was different because I ached for wanting, but it was not wanting for what the other Victoria girls had acquired. They were satisfied with the Art they got in England, but I could not be. Then I got Paris in my head, only I had no money left and no French language on my tongue, so I went home.

METCHOSIN PETUNIAS

Small smells them yet, those petunias of long ago, when Bigger, Middle, Small and Mary went summering on a farm in Metchosin. Mary was Bigger's friend. Bigger and Mary had touched twenty; Middle and Small had not left their teens behind.

There were not then as now countless summer cottages and cabins to be rented or owned by town dwellers. If children needed a place to recuperate after illness or while parents were having a dose of hospitalization, the healthy happiness of the Helgesens' farm out in Metchosin darted into people's brains and arrangements were made.

Mrs. Helgesen had a grown daughter Sara, whose rich singing voice made every farmer near weep round the Helgesen piano of an evening. Mr. and Mrs. Helgesen and Sara had bedrooms downstairs. Sara had three brothers, two grown to men, the third a fair-haired youngster and the pet of the family. The boys slept in a back attic room reached by an outer stair. The oldest boy had nightmares and broke his bed beating upon it with his fists, terrifying the whole household.

Our party had the whole upstairs front, consisting of a very large bedroom with two huge double beds, a sitting room and a balcony.

Bigger and Mary had one bed, Middle and I the other. Mary was very strict about our night behaviour. Nobody must talk after sleep began to touch our eyes. All clocks and watches were confiscated and shut out in the hall to tick themselves through the night alone. The door and the windows had to be just so.

The smell of the petunias in the garden below gave Mary rose-cold if they came into the room direct. But four persons sleeping in one room must have air, Mary admitted. She tolerated atmosphere filtered through our sitting room, where French windows opened onto a wide balcony running across the entire face of the house.

The great roofless balcony was a delight. From it you could look right into the petunias' faces and right up into the starry sky. Our rooms were very pleasant. We were extremely happy.

Mary was a Presbyterian parson's daughter, but she was also a joker. She always had a few minor ailments up her sleeve to steady her jokes and an appropriate text to temper the joke.

The farmhouse looked right down a long straight driveway. On either side were wide grain fields. A bathing beach was within walking distance; you could hear the sea washing and washing if the wind was in the right direction. Mrs. Helgesen was a kind hostess. They had horses, cows and pigs. There were always Mary's jokes and Sara's singing.

At times the big farm wagon was liberally spread with hay and we were bundled in and went for the most delightful picnics. The wagon bumped over the rough roads. When you came down bump, you looked on the floor to see if it was possible that there was more than a nosegay[1] of grasses to cushion you, it was so hard.

All these things Small remembers with delight, but what we ate

1. *bouquet*

or talked about or did she has forgotten. The thing she remembers, the thing that soaks right through all the Metchosin memories, is the smell of the petunias.

The farm's only bit of garden was a big round bed of petunias right in front of the house and below our windows. There was nothing in this bed but petunias, ordinary petunias, not goliath blossoms with fluted rims and fancy colours, but the old-fashioned pink and purple and white and a smell of such strength! Flowers grown from an ordinary 5-cent packet, unforced, unpampered, having come to full natural perfection and seeded. No other flowers mingled their scents with the petunias. The other scents, hay and farm smells, rode on cross-currents of air and did battle with the petunias. At noon the petunias' smell was hot and slightly wilting; the bed was in the full sunshine all day. In the early morning, when the trumpets were full of dew, the scent came moist and dainty. But on warm nights under a harvest moon with birds and chirping crickets stilled in the grain fields, who could stay in bed?

Not Small. Bigger slept, Mary slept, Middle slept; Small crept over Middle and slithered to the floor. She stole into the sitting room, drew a rocking chair in front of the open doors leading onto the balcony. The perfume of the petunias floated up. Small rocked herself to its smell. Her bare feet crept up the sill to the rough boards of the verandah. She leaned over the balcony rail and looked up at the moon and down at the petunias. The smell! The smell was Earth, Heaven and enchantment!

"Who's there? Who is rocking to and fro in our doorway! Wake, wake, girls, someone is in our sitting room," called Mary.

Bigger and Middle started up in bed.

"It's only me." Small's voice came from the sitting room.

"Small you silly child, get back to bed at once. What are you doing?"

"Only looking at the moon and the farm things, Bigger."

That was not quite all Small was doing. Small was storing, and for fifty years she was storing petunia smells. She has only to shut her eyes and tilt her nose to see and to smell those petunias years and years after they have blossomed. They open, blossom and are resown. Remembering the days when Bigger, Middle herself and a girl called Mary stayed at the old Helgesen farm at Metchosin.

STONE AND HEART

I don't know where it came from but there it was, an article with many uses in our kitchen. A straight-sided, narrow, smooth-faced stone, about ten inches long by three wide and two thick. You could crack nuts with it, drive a nail home, sharpen knives or break dog biscuits. It was kept on the kitchen window ledge in readiness should anyone require it for any purpose. Perhaps it had magic.

There was some special feel to this stone that made me love to handle it. Nobody could tell anything about the stone; even Father said he did not know where it came from. There was a sort of family politeness accorded to it not given to ordinary rock. I had heard it suggested that the stone was an old Indian weapon dug up when our land was cleared. One could easily imagine the cracking it could finish an enemy with.

The hammer in our house was always lost. I much preferred to hammer with the stone than with a flat hammer. Father preferred it to the slim shiny steel that belonged to the carving set.

Well it was after Father's death that the stone decided to take a hand in my affairs. Old Isabella, Father's great grapevine, missed him, for every day Father's long fingers used to pinch back and trim Isabella over the verandah and up round the upstairs window.

Now that Father was gone, one or another of us had to control her growing. One day I took the stone and the nail box and climbed the ladder, meaning to tack her up, but the dinner bell rang. I tumbled the stone into the gutter and went into the house, having the best intentions to finish training Isabella after lunch.

That afternoon we had a tennis party on our lawn and I thought no more of Isabella and the stone. Day crept down and down beneath the tall poplar trees.

"Hi there, Small!" shouted Middle from the group of young tennis players changing their tennis shoes on the verandah. "There's the stone peeping over the gutter, you better go and put her away. You know how grim the Elder is about it when she has forbidden your using it as a hammer."

"All right," as I disappeared round the house.

"Small! Small! I'll get it for you."

I knew the voice and already liked him, but did not heed. "Thinks girls can't climb ladders," I sneered to myself and was up gutter-high quick as a monkey before he was at the ladder base.

Then I descended the ladder face towards the house. Two rungs from the earth I was circled by a pair of strong arms.

"Miss Independence!" he said, as he lifted me down and turned me around.

"Oh!" I cried and the stone dropped from my hand into a tangle of peony bushes below. I lost something else that day, a perfectly whole good heart.

The old pact I had made with Elsie about kissing was broken like a bubble. Love rushed from nowhere and settled deep.

Soon I found the young man was only flirting with me, but too late, my heart was lost. It took fifteen years to pull myself out. Rooting it out was not half so hard as killing love, and when it was over

I could not see that anything was accomplished except a terrible amount of pain kept well under cover.

No one knew where the stone went; no one ever saw it again. I believe I was superstitious. I never hunted for it in earnest. It was heavy enough to bury itself quite deep. I wondered deeply, was it something electric pulled the stone into the garden soil and pulled my heart with it.

A FLANNEL PETTICOAT FOR A FELT HAT

There were two hotels a mile or two apart. One was good for sports-men but was considered loud for ladies. Middle-aged men with middle-aged wives stayed there. The other hotel was a farm and was more for families, a calm safe place surrounded by fields. Both were twenty miles from the nearest little town which was only a village. The farm hotel was on the river, the sporty hotel on the lake.

With two girl friends I was staying at the farm hotel. We had done the twenty bad miles on our bicycles and it had been a hard rough road, very hilly.

We used to row on the river but were warned not to go on to the lake, as its waters were subject to sudden severe storms and very dangerous. Besides, the sportsmen were always to be seen fishing there and, well, proper young ladies had better keep to the gentle river. Even Nature herself seemed to draw the line. The waters of the river were tree-shaded and vivid green. The waters of the lake were sky blue. Look up or look down, colour and property drew a sharp line.

One day we rowed up to the mouth of the river to see if we could actually touch the line that looked so clear a boundary. But when actually there we forgot our quest, because just near the river's mouth was a boatload of the sportsmen we were supposed to shun. With them were a middle-aged man and wife. The two boatloads exchanged stares. Then the middle-aged lady shouted across the river calling me by name. She was the mother of a girl pupil of mine. The boat from the lake came to the mouth of the river and the river boat went to the blue just inside the boundary of the lake. My pupil's mother said, "I do not fish and am lonely for company of my own sex and tired of sitting in boats all day hushed for fear of scaring fish. Please, my dears, come to the Lake Hotel and dine with me tomorrow night." We could walk round the road through the woods. They would bring us home by boat.

The dinner, good fish and grouse, then a wonderful row across the lake which happened to be smooth as the petal of a lily leaf. They told us they planned a long day's fishing next day, going far across the lake in a motor launch. They hoped the weather would be as fine as it promised, but you never could tell, this lake was moody. We did not see our friends again for nearly a week.

One evening as we were idling on our boat landing, we heard "Oooie," and a row boat turned into the river. In it were Mr. and Mrs. Sportsman. The lady was bursting news.

"We had an adventure," she said.

"Pouf, pouf!" said the man. "Nothing to speak of."

"Do tell us," we begged.

"Well," said Mrs. Sportsman. "First there was a storm and we nearly capsized. Then there was a bear. We had to land almost in the bear's mouth or the boat would have broken up on the rocks. It had to fairly fling us ashore and retire to a cove the boatman knew of round several points. Unfortunately there was no time to unload the food. We had neither lunch nor supper, only one dry match and the love letter of a young man who was very loath to part with it to start a fire. The bear watched us land on the flat rock."

"The hardest rock I ever sat on," said Mr. Sportsman.

"When we had undergone the shock of meeting the bear, the agony of seeing the boat dashing round the point not knowing if we would see boat or man again. The suspense of scratching our one match against the driest stick we could find, and had backed the bear into the bush by lighting the fire. We sat out the entire night cold and hungry."

"Pouf, pouf!" from Mr. Sportsman. "Nothing to be alarmed at. All that worried me was my wife's health, bronchitis you know, there was rain. Our point was exposed. I took off my felt hat and made my wife sit upon it."

She gave him a beamy smile.

"Ladies may not like to mention it. I must tell you, Flavia had already done her part, made a sacrifice for me, even while she chattered with cold. I wore at her insistence, pinned around my shoulders, her flannel petticoat—asthma and gout you know."

She nodded her head for what seemed like twenty minutes, though I don't suppose it was. I thought how lovely it was to see so devoted a couple.

"Do you know, Flavia, I am going to study natural history. You will never know the agony I endured all night pondering as to whether bears possess the same idiosyncrasy as bulls regarding scarlet."

"My darling," she whispered, "I exposed you all night to that torture! You looked so dreadfully wet with your hair trickling rain down your brow."

From our beds we were discussing the affair.

"Why did not the silly nuts each keep their own clothing," I said with a yawn.

The oldest of our trio said, "The point of the whole thing is love, my child, the satisfaction of self-sacrifice. Some day in a similar situation, you may exchange a flannel petticoat for a felt hat."

"If I do, and if he lets me, I hope the bear eats us both up."

MAUDE

Maude was a thoroughbred chestnut mare, and beautiful. My oldest sister owned Maude and allowed me to ride her. I was just home from three years at the San Francisco Art School, restless and lonely. Mounted on Maude, I forgot everything except perfect happiness. Beyond the town I flew along the country roads on Maude.

I had camped on a sketching trip seven miles out of the city the week before, and found when I returned home that I had lost my watch. I mounted Maude and went to my old camping ground to seek it.

Maude stood higher than our old horse Johnny. I forgot that and miscalculated in dismounting—I fell. The bridle slipped from my hand. I lay flat on the ground beside the mare. One boot was tight caught in the stirrup. I rode a Mexican saddle and wore a long heavy divided skirt which came to my boot-soles; this was scandal enough for Victoria! No woman had ridden cross-saddle here before.

When I did not get up but hung heavily from the stirrup Maude began to tremble. The sensitive creature knew there was trouble. I undid the fastening of the skirt about my waist, hoping to release my boot. I tugged and strained, but my boot only slipped entirely through the stirrup. Very gently, the frightened mare began to prance.

With every movement I was drawn closer in, till my head was pillowed on her hind hoof, and I was utterly at her unguided mercy.

Far above me the tree tops were waving and above again was the blue sky. Immediately above me was the belly of the horse.

"Maude, Maude I do not want to die! I am young. Don't kick my brains out, don't drag me to be broken on the jagged stumps, or tear me through the brush to have my eyes ripped out. Maude, Maude!" Each time I called her name I felt her quiver.

I had passed a rig upon the road, soon it would turn into the lane. My dog had rushed to the familiar stream to drink. When the rig passed he would tear up and bark, used as he was to guarding this camping ground. What would Maude do then, bewildered and without guidance?

I heard the rig on the road.

"Steady, girl, good Maude—please!"

She turned her head and the trembling stopped. Her fine ears were pricked; she too had heard the rig. We could not see the road, there was thick bush between. Gently the mare slipped her hoof from under my head. I felt her gather herself to leap. She sprang forward and upward with a movement sure and dainty as a deer. The stirrup flung my boot free. Clearing my head by a couple of inches, she bounded into the deep wood.

I lay still. The rig passed. The dog came back and stood over me, whimpering.

"Maude," I cried and from the wood. The mare whinnied and came to me.

I caught the bridle rein and remounted. I had been near to death or maiming, but for your gentle wisdom, Maude.

SMASH

Middle and I were childhood chums. We shared everything. To be sure, she was all for doll mothering, while I preferred pups and kittens. Middle was studious and went through school with honourable mentions and things like that, while I squeezed through and obtained many goose eggs, especially on my arithmetic papers. By-and-by I went away to study art, but all the while I kept up a furious correspondence with Middle. I imagined Middle and I would always go on like that, keeping close all our lives.

When I came back from the Art School I did notice a subtle change had come. Was it her fault or mine or growth, I pondered, or were our interests in life widening? She had made new friends, so had I, but mine were in California.

One day after school I was exercising our old horse Johnny along Moss Street. This was a favourite street of mine. At that time it was all pure country down to its sea end. Upper Moss Street was rather snob where it joined Fort. The Fort Street end was quite high; the level became lower and lower as it approached the sea. Both sides of Moss Street were one tangle of broom bushes and wild roses, which scratched buggies, but colour and scent—oh my!

Not far from the sea end, I noticed a little picket gate inserted in a plain rail fence. On the gate was a notice board, "The Hermitage" and beneath in smaller letters, "To Let." Inside the picket gate was a sizeable field of rough grass with a little worn path ending in a grove of pine trees. Through the trees showed little broken glimpses of a house.

I dismounted and throwing the bridle rein across the pickets of the gate, I opened and entered. The house was small, its colour drab. It was an up and down home with stairs. Without the "Hermitage" on the gate you would know it had been the home of a bachelor. It was not womanish in any way. I peeped into all the windows I could reach. One could be cosy here with fires going and some sort of life about. The only life apparent was black cawing crows. They were nesting in the little grove of tall pines and noisily resented my intrusion. I wondered why the bachelor left—loneliness?

"I'd love to live in this little house," I thought, "Just Middle and I together." One room facing north, a biggish window, the studio I planned. I could paint there. When I looked back from the gate, dusk had quite sucked the house into the grove, and the crows had stopped cawing and gone back to mothering.

Middle and I, what fun! That night when, as usual, Middle and I sat up in bed to munch our apples in the dark, I said, "Middle, I've found the loveliest house for you and me." I told her all about The Hermitage.

Middle frowned tremendously. She said, "I don't want to live in your old hermitage! What would I be doing while you painted?"

"Whatever you wanted. Just live and boss and housekeeping! I'll help with the work of course. Wouldn't you like it, Middle?"

"Crows and the muddle and messed paint? I would not . . . your housekeeper!"

Her tone was smashing. Crash! Our ways had parted! Middle had never hinted that she planned a career of her own. I never again looked through the bars and pickets of The Hermitage when I rode that way.

HOMECOMING

Small was still the youngest but she wasn't the littlest any more. She now had a studio home of her own in Vancouver, while her sisters Elder, Bigger and Middle all lived in the old home in Victoria.

Bigger was polishing the top of the sewing machine. Not that it needed polishing, for its lustre was so high and so deep that you could almost see that faithful family slave that had made all the little girls' dresses and now made their woman dresses, right through the lid. But Bigger was like that, she polished things till you were afraid to breathe for fear they would tarnish.

Middle came in with a quiet shininess about her like still water. "I'm going to the boat now. Elder has started, she said she'd drive me, but I'm quicker footed than her old nag," she laughed.

"You'll be able to carry the overflow," sniffed Bigger. "I suppose she's bringing them all. It will be dirt, smells and screeches till the Christmas holidays are over. I kind of wish I hadn't house cleaned till after Christmas," she reflected.

"Well," replied Middle, "You know she couldn't have all that sort of thing while she lived here, so I suppose it's natural she should burst forth now she has her own home."

Bigger dusted Auntie's already dustless photo on the mantelpiece and muttered again, "Dirt, smell and screeches." All the same there was a twinkle in her naturally bright eyes, and the wisp of a smile played across her mouth. It would be nice to be together for Christmas even if Small's extras had to be included.

The old horse lumbered up with the phaeton.[1] Elder's face beamed above her bonnet strings. From the feet to the waist, Small was obscured by a shaggy sheep dog, from the waist to the top of her head by wicker baskets. Middle came in the gate carrying a bird cage enveloped in cloth wrappings.

"Oh, I say, be careful of that," shouted Small from her obscurity. "Peggy had a family last night. They're in the coconut shell."

Middle peeked under the cover. "Horrors!" she exclaimed, "It's rats! I thought It was the bullfinches I was carrying. What's the revolting thing in the corner?"

"Oh, that's Peter. Papa rats eat their offspring sometimes, so I tied him up in a stocking. I'll take him out, the poor darling must feel so stuffy."

Middle dropped the cage with a disgusted, "Ugh!"

"Here, take the girls," said Small, handing out the two baskets.

Bigger took them gingerly. "Sure there's no snakes?" she asked.

"No, there isn't, you boob, it's the parrots."

Just to prove it, a lemon-crested cockatoo shot her head out of a hole she had industriously made on the journey and said sweetly, "Sally's a Sally."

"Ha ha ha!" screeched a grating voice from the other basket. "Oh, you old fool!"

"I don't really think it is nice," began Bigger.

"Oh it was such fun," broke in Small. "She said that to a parson on board and he thought it was me."

1. Phaeton: *a light 4-wheeled open carriage.*

"I hope it was no one we know," said Elder.

"That reminds me, quick let me to the tap!" cried Small, leaping over the rat cage and the parrot baskets. "An old fool woman knocked my bag over. I had no idea till a man tapped me on the shoulder and said, 'Excuse me, Madam, there is a fish flapping round under your seat.'"

She had reached the garden tap now and was extracting a jar from the bag on her arm. Two goldfish flapped at the bottom of the jar in a dribble of water. "Poor lambs," said Small, "hope you did not get too dry."

Next she uncovered the rat's cage. From a hole in the top Peter's long pink nose protruded and bunches of white fur. Small enlarged a hole and extracted Peter from the stocking, slipping him into the pocket of her coat with a pat. Bigger and Middle shivered.

Billie the sheep dog watched every move his mistress made.

Elder, who was climbing out of the phaeton, gave a violent shriek. "Oh, oh somebody catch my poor Ben! Billie will kill him sure. Oh, oh somebody quick! My poor old Benny!"

A decrepit old fox terrier was bristling peevishly out of the house. The big sheep dog regarded him scornfully.

"Ben, Ben!" shouted his mistress as he made a dash at the wooly sheep dog.

"To heel, Billie," said Small quietly. The dog obeyed and Elder bore her veteran to the house in a palpitating frenzy at not being allowed to work up a scrap.

Everybody climbed the steps of the house. On the threshold Bigger turned, "Don't let Billie in the house, the floor has just been polished," she said.

They entered into the sitting room.

"Don't let the parrots sit on the chair backs, they've just been done up," said Elder.

"Please don't stand that wet fish jar on the machine top," said Bigger.

"Don't let the rats out please please!" they all shouted together.

"Don't don't don't!!" thundered Small. "What can we do do do?"

Picking up Auntie's photograph she made a face at it. "Insulted me with cotton flannel rompers on my eighth birthday, you did," she said and turned the photo to the wall.

"You ought to be ashamed," said Bigger.

"How can you behave so," said Elder.

Middle just grinned.

From her basket came the voice of Sally the cockatoo. "Sally's a Sally!" she said, with a gentle voice as if stating a fact—something that was and was completely satisfactory. Then she made the sound of kissing. Everybody laughed.

"You bet you're a Sally, my blessing," answered Small, opening the baskets. Both birds beaked their way out and fell to preening themselves.

Small looked around the room for something that wasn't polished and sat herself down a moment in the old praying chair. "How I did long for them when I was the littlest girl," she said. Then she jumped up and started settling her family in corners of the old home that were safe from "don'ts" and the Christmas preparations fired ahead.

NOOTKA HAD A HOTEL

The Nootka Hotel was not much of a place but it was all the hotel Nootka had. So you had to put up with it if you had business in these parts and had to wait over boats. It was a long, narrow frame building that straddled a gully. There was a door at one end, and the approach to the door was three planks elevated on stilts. The Nootka Hotel was like nothing. Queer people came and went, ate and slept, like the mixed breeds in an old fowl yard.

The hotel was run by a woman with a girl child of six. Maybe the woman was wholly a widow, maybe not, maybe she was just widowed on and off. It was none of my business what she was; but I noticed that I, the only woman boarder, was not so readily attended to, nor so graciously served, as the men. The beds went unmade till late afternoon and the food came mostly out of tin cans.

The reason for Nootka's existence was a big fish cannery with the usual setting, the usual smells. The most characteristic of these was the separate villages for the separate nationalities. There was the big Indian village over the mud flats, with cabins in a long row and a wide plank walk before them. The fish company provided a one-room cabin and a cook stove for each family, every thing else they brought in bundles and strewed them all over the floor. In off hours from the canneries, the Indians squatted on the broad plank walk in front of the cabins. Why the babies did not run splinters into their stomachs or fall off the platform into the mud I can't imagine. The hut doors stood open, absorbing British Columbia. This was the Indian's native environment.

In the little settlements closer to the hotel, the workers were aliens. Set back along the pines was a great raw frame building. This was where the Norwegians lived. Below them was the little Jap village neat as a pin, with little flowers and green things growing in pots. Up the gully was a gaunt three-story frame building, the Chinese boarding house. Tatters of derelict curtains hung at the windows, and the doors and windows were tight shut. In the cannery these people worked together. Outside, each kind kept severely apart.

The cannery boss had a nice new house. Bookkeepers, engineers, timekeepers and clerks did the best they could in shacks and odd rented rooms, and fed in the hotel. The population of Nootka was as seasonable as the weather; all depended on what the fish did.

Nootka, like all coast cannery towns, straggled along the water's edge. Behind the town was dense forest, well-timbered and heavily undergrowthed. There was only one made path through the forest. It ran to I don't know where; besides that path there were only deer trails.

I went into the forest to paint. It was desperately lonesome and silent—until suddenly, a man came crushing through the undergrowth. He halted almost on top of me, as tremendously astonished to see me as I to see him.

"One lady, she paint, this wood? So?" he cried, astounded, in halting broken English.

His astonishment annoyed me, as the sudden appearance of him had jittered me. Why should I not paint? I hated being watched and spoken to when I painted. I was restless and cross under his scrutiny, so he turned into the bush. Then I was ashamed. The creature did not know I was as indigenous to these woods as a pine tree. He was a curious-looking being, tin cans suspended by strings to all parts of his person, full tins dangling heavily and paper cups flapping light. In his arms he carried other parcels.

Later I learned that he was a Russian who had pre-empted a section of land far back up a creek. He had created a vegetable garden in the forest and had intended to sell his produce in Nootka. But he was nervous of the open sea and his outmotor boat. Instead of using the boat he trudged seven or eight weary miles through the rough forest trail and carried his provisions home on his own back. He lived on that and his garden. Then I was sorry that I had not stopped my work a minute and been gracious to the solitary creature.

Nootka Hotel offended all my five senses, but the summit of my indignation was reached the night the woman stood up in the middle of the dining room and announced, "No food will be served in this dining room tomorrow. I go picnicking. Those guests wishing to do so may help themselves from the larder."

I came downstairs the next morning not knowing what to expect, and found my usual tea and toast, better made than usual. I had no idea how many permanents we numbered. As I left the room, a man somewhere in the middle of man's normal span of life accosted me.

"Well today there's only me an you. Gosh! Look at them flies. I'll up to the cannery cook house, that Chink is a fine chap. Like steak? I can cook steak fine."

"But she left the job to both of us, shan't I help?"

"When you are through your work, dinner will be served."

He had such nice teeth. More than his kindness in cooking for me was the fact that he recognized my painting as a serious work. Most of these people just laughed and considered me a dauber playing about in the woods.

We ate together, and the steak was well-cooked. I knew a lot more about Nootka's queer people after dinner than before. His comment was always kindly.

At my disgusted reference to our hostess' casualness in running her hotel he said, "Well, she is a casual piece but good enough at heart."

"If she professes to run a hotel, she should do it."

He shrugged. "Home runnin' aint in some wimmin. Ye jest carn't larn 'em all."

Perhaps he was speaking from experience, perhaps that was why our steak was so perfectly cooked: his woman had been one of the ones you couldn't "larn."

SMOKING WITH THE COW

To have an index finger wagged right in your face, throbbing the air eighteen inches from your nose, has always infuriated me and always will.

"You mark my words Miss! There is not going to be any smoking in my house." Wag, wag of the finger. "Disgusting, unlady-like. Fast. No Carr man that I know has smoked and no Carr woman shall as long as I have a say in this house. If, having picked the vice up abroad, smoke you must, then go to the stable and smoke with the cow. If other Carr women have managed without smoke, you can."

The Elder turned on her heel and left the room. "I told you so," came through the open door. I didn't know Bigger was sitting there listening to Elder's words and praying. Between them they always tried to make me feel the low, lower and lowest Carr.

I had learned to smoke while at the London art school. English girls did, Canadian girl had not yet acquired the custom. Nearly all the girls in the Westminster Art School smoked and thought me stupid because I didn't care to learn. Then, when I was ill, the doctor said, "Smoking would help your nerves," then I smoked, but not to excess.

It had not become an obsession with me; the fuss they were making about it put my back up. I did like my smoke when I was thinking over my work and I did not see why I should not. This was the first cigarette which I had smoked in the week I was home. It had been the equivalent of a bomb flung into my family's bosom. I accepted their ultimatum.

As I made my way to the cow-yard, I met Bong with a great pail of milk. That meant the cow was at home. "Halloo cow, I am coming to keep you company." Lifting Bong's milking stool from its peg, I pressed against the chewing beast and, leaning my head against her shoulder, I smoked in peace. Why not? She kept curving her thick neck over her shoulder and giving my hair a slight friendly lick.

ONE GOOD TIME

Susan the Indian used to come, and her sister Mary with her, to our house selling clams and bundles of pitch wood for the lighting of fires. Mary was tall and dignified, but Susan was gruff and taciturn. If you gave them a cup of tea, she snatched it without "thank you," while Mary smiled and said, "Tank."

Mary wore a black silk handkerchief over her smooth parted hair; her long plaits gathered behind her ears. The part, starting at her forehead, went to the nape of her neck. The hair, beginning in two great swollen plaits, dwindled until a string tied them together across her shoulders, each plait no thicker than a pencil. Susan wore a yellow handkerchief, bound untidily round her shock of un-combed hair which stuck out, cut half-short because she had been in jail. They cut Indian women's hair in jail.

One day Susan came alone. Mary had become tubercular and died. Susan told us with unlively stoical gruffness, acting the cough, the moans of weakness and loneliness, but you felt her great hurt underneath. She would not show it.

By and by Susan stopped coming. I did not know where she lived, beyond that she was not a Songhees Indian. The Songhees

Reserve used to be on the Victoria harbour. It had been bartered for a fine site on Esquimalt harbour, as the Victoria site was required for industrial purposes.

Occasionally I would spend a day on the reserve, carrying a sandwich-lunch and sketching and visiting among the people. One day in a little mean shanty set back from the rest, a woman sat on the floor weaving a mat. I stopped to chat with her just because she was an Indian and—

"It's Susan!" I cried.

"Uh-huh me."

"You have not been for a long time, no clams, no gum stick!"

"Me bloke, steam car steal my leg."

I saw then that there was only one bare foot sticking beyond the pink print skirt, and that a crude home-made crutch lay beside her. I remembered reading in the paper that a drunken Indian woman had gone to sleep on the railway track and a freight train had cut off her leg.

"Poor Susan!"

"Me no walk'm, this one no me now." She patted the stump.

"Poor Susan!"

She went straight on weaving as she talked. Dipping her fingers in a pan of water, she selected a strand of inner cedar-bark from a bundle beside her, moistening the bark, pinching the end between her strong yellow teeth. With her horny fingernail, she split the strand from top to bottom exactly the width of all the other strands in her pan.

"Have you a finished mat Susan? I want to buy."

"Uh-huh." She pointed with her crutch to a dark corner where neatly rolled her mats lay, and neatly piled her baskets stood. For no matter how muddlesome and untidy the rest of an Indian hut was, their work and their work-material was always kept tidy and clean. I took the mat, admired it, and laid its price beside her.

"Did the railway give you money for your leg, Susan?"

"Injun Agent pay sick house . . . Lailway say, spose Injun stlaight, lailway pay as for leg . . . Lailway say, spose dlunk injun hurted, no matter pay . . . Pliceman say, Injun dlunk, Injun pay a fine, too . . . Injun dlunk, Pliceman take just same money for leg, for make fine . . . Tlain take leg from Injun all same as fine."

Susan was paying, would pay, for the rest of her life for a great, grand drunk. The very memory yet created a great grin.

"No matter," she smiled up at me, "me have one good time."

PRAYERS AND PICKLES

The Presbyterian parson was dignified enough. He stood at the head of the rough board table covered with worn oilcloth; a coal-oil lamp hung over the table and smelt. Down the centre of the long table were "the perennials" sequencing in rotations: cruets, pickle jar, a delft mug of assorted spoons and a receptacle of toothpicks. Stews, vegetables, pies came and went; the central cruet, pickles, spoon-mug, toothpicks stuck faithful to their regular places, equally spaced at intervals down the long narrow table's centre. It saved much passing.

Down each side of the table ran a splintery bench. One end of the table was against the wall, at the other end was a chair for the most important guest. Tonight the parson occupied the chair and gave a blessing. He had eaten a good dinner; now he stood up and invited those who would to remain and join in the service he was about to conduct. He was not the parson of White Skidegate, he was the missionary for Indian Skidegate, three miles away. White Skidegate was a huddle of cabins, the whale-oil refinery and Mrs. Fraser's hotel. The Indians probably had an Indian name for their own village.

The weekly coast steamer called at White Skidegate regularly and was due somewhere between midnight and noon. Fishermen, loggers and owners of little lost holdings along the shoreline came hoping for mail and certain of a good dinner at Mrs. Fraser's Hotel. Having invited us, the parson turned around and invited another long table, the twin of ours across the room, to move over and participate. This sent some of them flying out the door; a few stayed.

Mrs. Fraser and her kitchen help put on clean aprons and took their places on the benches as soon as the soiled cups and plates had been hurried into the kitchen. We condensed as much as possible. Those on the back bench against the wall remained as they were; those facing them threw their legs over the bench and backed the wall-worshippers. It make them feel more "churchy" to all face one way, and it made the splintery seats feel more pewish even if you splintered your leg. We massed pretty close, shuffling at half-sit down the rough bench, to make room for those of the other table and for Mrs. Fraser and her help.

There was a prayer, bible reading, a higgledy-piggledy hymn that no one knew, then an address from the parson. Followed by a long pause, broken by His Reverence inviting—"Brother Gow, will you lead us in prayer?"

Edna, the girl called in to chaperone me at the parsonage in the Indian Village during the absence of the parson's women folk and who was my guest for the night, kicked my shin. "Prepare for anything!" she whispered in my ear, "Sit steady!"

Brother Gow arose: he was immediately behind me. I felt his overwhelming enormousness and hot breath down my neck. Only the narrow table was between us; his bent head sent his voice rushing over the crown of my head like a hot bath. He began by pounding his great fist down on the table and dictatorially shouting, "God!" as if he were arresting someone making off around the corner.

After his great shout, he began to wheedle, to cajole. Presently however, he got firmer with God, ordering this and that, stating our desires, our requirements. His voice gained volume; soon it was a bellow, a roar. He touched on weather, on fishing, food and clothing; first entreating, then demanding, finally threatening the Almighty how we were going to act if our demands were not met. At every threat his fist came down on the table and the pickle-jars jumped, slopping their vinegar.

Everyone held their breath. At last, the biggest pickle-jar overturned. Edna and I heard the gush of pickle liquid crossing the oilcloth and moved as far apart as the neighbours on our other sides would permit, to allow the rush of vinegar, onions and baby cucumbers to tumble from table to bench from bench, to floor, rolling and trickling.

"Amen!" shouted brother Gow with final awfulness. The oilcloth was strewn with sprigs of pickled cauliflower which could not roll like onions and cucumbers.

The parson raised his hands and pronounced a quiet blessing. Mrs. Fraser rushed to the kitchen for a cloth, the Indian maid for a dustpan and brush with which to chase pickles and onions all over the floor.

At last, I dared look behind to see what manner of man Gow was—externally medium. He was mopping his brow and hands with a great red and yellow bandana. The wrestle with God had exhausted the man.

Outside, God's night was perfectly still and the moon smiled. She was calming, after the ferocity of Brother Gow's tirade among hot dinner smells. We went gladly into the open cool.

ADOLPHUS

I wish I might die as politely and as beautifully as my old Persian cat Dolf.[1] Fulfilling a complete span of cat years he kept his grand silver body in perfect shape to the end—sight unimpaired, hearing unimpaired, the sleek shine of his coat fluffing free and well-tended, not one hair of it diminished from its original density. His teeth were gone, they fell out naturally of their own accord—no dentist, no dentures. When his gums lacked grip for mousing, they nibbled contentedly on bread and milk, chopped liver and top milk; then his work was done. He sat in the sun and purred to capacity. His loving strengthened with age and it centred on me. To the rest of the human world he was indifferent, though he was true pals with his contemporaries, my bobtail sheepdogs.

He was reared among the sheepdogs and acquired many of their staunch noble qualities. When we walked in Beacon Hill Park, he followed among them. If a stranger came, he climbed a tree and waited for them to pass. One thing he did not acquire from them was the typical bobtail shambling gait. He kept his own aerial grace and dig-

1. Adolphus *was the cat's full name. The events of this story appear in a shorter story in* Heart of A Peacock, *titled, "Woo Saves Dolf." (Woo was Emily's monkey)*

nity. When he walked among them he was like a ship in full sail among a company of scows.

One night I found him upon my stairs. He made no response to my caresses; his eyes stared, no green showed, only two enlarged black pupils. A dark brown fluid was trickling from his mouth. I kept him by my bedside all night, and all night he stared with the same black unconscious eyes. I dosed him and he took patiently what I put down his throat. It was too late to send for the elderly Veterinary who tended my creatures, but in the morning I sent.

The Veterinary said, "This cat has been poisoned." He said I had done all that was possible through the night, but now the cat's heart was almost done from strychnine. His only chance was half a teaspoonful of brandy in water every hour. The cat and I carried out instructions faithfully. He did not like the brandy but suffered me to put it in his mouth and he swallowed and recovered. He had absolute faith in my ministrations.

"That is a noble cat," said the Veterinary. "It would have been a pity had he died." But Dolf had a tremendous grip on life, the cat's nine lives and then some more.

When he was ten years old he was run over by an automobile. Too crushed to make home, he lay under a bush outside my property while I searched and called. After four days I found him, or rather my monkey did.

It was like picking up an empty skin. He was so emaciated, mashed to a jelly and unconscious. I carried him home and laid him on a pillow. As I had no brandy in the house I smeared cream on his parched and lolling tongue. After a while he drew his tongue in and swallowed. I sent for the Vet.

"Kill Dolf!" I ordered.

The Veterinary made careful examination. "Any ordinary cat, yes, but not Dolf. There are no bones broken. He is just crushed. He'll recover."

"I do not want him to suffer."

"You cannot make a suffering cat purr. I have watched the cat while examining him. Whenever you were near, when your hand was within reach he stretched to rub his cheek on it and purred every time you touched him. Give him a chance; it means care and trouble. It's nursing will do it, not physic."

"He shall have nursing," I said. I carried him to the garden and laid him in a little hollow in the warm earth under the lilac bush, a spot he loved. The sun played in and out among the lilac blossoms and over Dolf's broken silver-coated body. I massaged his bruised flesh and felt it firm up day by day. He made complete recovery and lived for eight years after that, dying at the fine old age of eighteen years.

Dolf died in the most polite, unfussy and beautifully kind way I know. He went in a day. Lay in the yard and slept out, no moans, apparently no suffering, his death just as satisfactory as his life. I should like to die like my cat.

"HE", "SHE" AND THE RAM

"He" and "She" loved each other thoroughly and fought furiously. The way of their loving was snarly as a couple of tomcats on a fence venting their fury in agonized shrieks, ears laid flat, lips curled back. The crouching creatures stood five or six feet apart on the fence rail quivering, but neither blood spilt nor fur flew, just noise.

The woman spoke of the man always as "He." The man spoke of the woman as "She." When the pair conversed they called each other, "You." They owned a wild farm of untamed wide acreage. Each had their own special hobby. His hobby was prize sheep, hers a kennel of Boston Terriers. They had a comfortable house. There were dogs bedded in every corner. Over all their wild-brush acreage his sheep roamed free.

A shallow ravine ran through the property. It was crossed by a little bridge of planks. On the opposite side of the ravine to the old couple's house was a two-room cottage which they used as a guest house and which they lent to me once for sketching. I went there to paint, taking with me a small monkey and my griffon dogs. We were fortunately out of hearing of their old people's quarrels. When I went over the ravine to them, they were so interested in my monkey they forgot to fight.

The day before my taking possession of the cottage, the old man's sheep had returned from the Fall Fair where they had won many prizes. The pride of his flock was a young ram which had taken first in every class. He was too young to compete for champion this year. He stood in line to become grand champion next. The old lady was as proud as Punch at "His" success.

Early the next morning she came rushing across the ravine. "The prospective champion is ailing! 'He' is nearly crazy. I am downright sorry for him," "She" said, her *He*'s, *She*'s and *Him*'s getting me muddled.

"What ails the ram?"

"That's the trouble. It has the same symptoms as the ram 'He' lost two days after last year's show, and we suspect foul play. You see 'He' has an enemy who also shows sheep. The enemy was furious at us, his own ram being beaten. He was heard to say, he'd 'see to it our ram was not eligible for the championship next year.' He was smart enough to leave no trace of what he did, but that boasted threat, and two years running the same perplexing symptoms . . . look suspicious."

"Have you sent for the Vet?"

"Yes, but we are twenty miles from town. He cannot get here till late afternoon, in the meantime . . . "

"What did he prescribe for the other ram?"

"Hot fomentations."[1]

"Why not try the same this time?"

"How can I? 'He's' up in the barn crying, helpless as a baby. Barn is a quarter of a mile from the house. My legs won't do it! I tell you!

---

1. Fomentation: *to wrap, rub or press a loose textured fabric (such as flannel) soaked in hot water, medicated or not, to the surface of the body.*

Even if they would, the fomentations would be cold and no good after travelling that distance from cook stove to ram's stomach."

"I'll help. If we cannot carry the mountain to Mohammed let's carry Mohammed to the cook-stove! Can the creature walk?"

"With 'His' help."

"Tell him to start at once and lead the ram down."

"She" bustled back to the house and I put on a big apron. Then we turned out a small woodshed just outside the kitchen door.

They were a pathetic pair, the red-eyed bent old man and the ram dazed with suffering. The man's dirt-engrained hand rested on the ram's hanging head. We tied the ram in the least-draughty corner of the shed.

"Aw, Billie!" Every time "He" voiced the ram's name, the sick beast half turned his pathetic head, but his eyes remained shut, heavy with sickness.

The old lady urged the cook stove to a roar. The old man sat upon the chopping block hugging his own arms and murmuring, "Aw, Billie! Aw, Billie!"

I shoved the apple box under the stomach of the ram and sat down on it. "She" brought the hot packs smoking from the kitchen stove and laid them across my arms. I spread my arms under the ram holding the packs close to him. The ram stood, hopelessly patient. We went on hour after hour.

At long last the Vet came. He said we could not have done better but we had done it in the hardest way. He filled the packs with hot bran sprinkled them with turpentine and improvised an over-all of sacking to hold the packs in place so as to relieve my aching arms. He gave the animal some medicine and held out hope. We were to keep reheating the packs well on into the night; he would come tomorrow.

Billie seemed easier. He lay down and slept, tired with pain. We were weary too. The old man sat the night through in the wood shed. I was sure the ram was going to live. I had held the packs long enough to the patient beast to begin to love him and to have a heart-felt interest in his case. One had to admire his dignity even in suffering, apart from my fondness for "He" and "She." It was late when I crossed the dark ravine to go to bed in my cottage.

In the morning I ran across the ravine, hopes high. The ram turned his head at the opening of the door. He began chafing his woolly side against the wall of the shed. "He" held a posy of fresh clover in his hand and was sitting on the apple box close beside his ram.

"He" said, "Won't ye eat. Won't ye eat none, Billie?" looking rue-fully at the clover in his hand.

"Looks better, don't you think? or not?"

The ram opened his eyes and gave a yearning bleat.

"Wants the open," said "He." "All right Billy, I'll help ye."

The ram's legs were weak, he tottered. The old man crouched and threw his arms across the great wide back of the ram, guiding him to a shady spot under a tree. The ram lay down.

The old man started off.

"Where are you going?" "She" called.

"To hunt him some Oregon grape, the young shoots is very chewsome to sheep."

"They would not appeal to me as an invalid diet," "She" remarked with impatience. "Maybe Billie's taste is different to mine."

With the return of hope there was a slight ring of asperity in her voice.

The ram's head sank and sank till it rested on the earth. He seemed to rest easy. When his master returned with the tender shoots (too young to be prickly) he bent over the creature, held the green to his lips. Billy did not heed. "Asleep I guess." The old man sat, sagged and hopeless on a nearby log.

"She" and I went to our respective house jobs.

I saw the Vet drive into the gate. I stayed my side of the ravine. The quiet of Sunday was all about. I was nearly asleep when "She" came into my room. She did not speak but put her arms on the table and her head down on her arms and cried, "Poor boy! Poor boy! 'He's' broke."

"Billie?" I could not picture, "He" as having ever been a boy.

"No, my husband. The ram is dead. The vet is helping to dig a pit to bury him in. The pride of his flock destroyed for spite last year. The pride of his flock destroyed again this year all, all for spite! 'He' says he is giving up sheep. Poor boy! Poor old boy!" "She" dried her eyes. I got up. "Come over, I've made coffee. There is nothing 'He' enjoys like coffee, strong an' well sugared."

There was a new earth mound not far from the back door. The two men were at the table talking of everything but sheep.

"She" filled their coffee cups and filled one for me. "She" did not fill one for herself but hovered about "Him," filling and refilling his cup.

"He" wanted to look something up in a paper and put on his spectacles.

"Pesky no good specks!" "He" tried to adjust them.

"She" slipped those from off her own nose. "Here y'are. Mine suit him best," "She" laughed, half ashamed of her weakness. "Paid fifteen dollars for his, 'He' did. I got mine at the fifteen-cent store. Fifteen cent specks is best!" I had heard them wrangling over the spectacles ever since I had arrived at the farm, both wanted the fifteen cent ones.

"Seems like thoroughbreds don't pay, not even in specks. I'm a-goin' in for mutton, Mother!" he said it a little ruefully. "She" laid her hand on his arm.

The Vet and I looked out of the window and talked weather. Under our talk we heard "Poor old boy! Poor old boy!" as though "She" was speaking to our shoes under the table.

"Was it two firsts ye took on that pup Mother? Been too busy since show to heed much?"

"Maybe."

ONLY THE TRUSTWORTHY

He was an unwanted baby, doubly unwanted because he was a twin. Harry was adopted from an orphanage by an old woman, who died when he was only a lad. The old woman had been a missionary in the far North. Then her family would not keep him. The lad was pushed from one to the other of the woman's people. They obviously loathed him. He was mentally deficient, an unattractive youth. For a while he lived alone in a little cabin in the woods, picking up this and that few cents for doing some trifling job inefficiently, or they gave him food for charity's sake. At last they sent him south to a town where his only living relative lived. But the relative was married and there were half-grown impressionable children in the home.

The boy became unmanageable. It was not fair to anybody. He could not earn a living. He could not care for himself. The only solution was the Provincial Asylum. It was grim, but there he would have kindness and care. He was now thirty-five years old. In a few things he was rational, but in most things he was foolish, with just enough sense to realize that he had none.

The Asylum was far out. The relative was a busy woman. I decided I would make it my job to go at regular intervals to see Harry. He was bitterly resentful at having been put where he was. He wanted freedom. On fine summer days, if he had been behaving well, I was allowed to take him into the grounds. He took great pride and pleasure in showing me about his conservatory, his rabbitry, his ponds of fancy water fowl, his monkey, his chickens, his flower beds. Suddenly he would remember and beg, "Get me out, I'm a prisoner!"

The sensiblest lunatics were working in the grounds. There were always keepers watching. I could not always distinguish the keepers from the looneys, except that the lunatics laughed more. Harry took me to see the laundries. Here there were the most jovial lunatics. I sat on a tub between two who roared with laughter the whole time; they seemed to expect it of me so I roared too and so did Harry. Then we went to the workshop, a rambling building where the better patients did any work they were capable of doing. A young man with a beautiful face was sewing on a sewing machine, making clothes; others were doing bits of carpentry or darning socks or knitting. There were not a great many patients in the workshop.

Harry said, "This is Jacob the Indian, he is very anxious to see you because I told him you had been to Queen Charlotte Islands, that is where he comes from."

I shook hands with the Indian and admired the little totem pole he was carving. He had a shelf full of them, poorly carved, but they gave him occupation and happiness.

"Shall I play for you?" he said when I had seen his carvings.

"Please do."

From among the totem poles on his shelf he took a squeaky violin and writhed cryings out of her.

I shook hands with keepers and lunatics, quite at sea as to which were which, and then Harry and I sat on a bench in the garden.

The day was hot. I had brought some chocolates in a paper bag;

everything had to pass inspection in the office before you gave it to a patient. The sun shone on the paper bag, and the chocolate ran round liquid in the bottom of the bag. While Harry talked he kept dipping the tips of his fingers in the liquid and bringing them out chocolate coated. His hands were ghastly yellow, which the brown chocolate accentuated. He held them up and licked the sweetness off the tips of his fingers. It was nice to sit in the quiet after being shown off like a little boy's school prize in workshop and laundry.

In the winter or on cold days I was entertained in the visitor's room, a long room on the top floor where the board held their meetings, a bleak bare place with heavily barred windows and a long table down the centre of the room. Sometimes I was the only visitor, sometimes there were other lunatics entertaining a wife or sister. Harry told me in loud whispers who they were.

"The man at the end of the room has been an organist, he writes lovely poetry too. He would write some for you if you liked. That is his wife visiting with him."

She looked very unhappy. The man paid little attention to her. (I suppose it was another case of resentment at being shut up.) She had brought him oranges and some picture magazines. He turned his back on her, and ran through the picture books with great boredom. I noticed he held them upside down.

Presently he got up and came heavily over to Harry, shoving the oranges and the magazines into his hands, "Here you can have them, I don't want her things."

The wife later told me, when we walked back to the bus together, "It is so difficult knowing what will please them, what to take. They have very good food, very good care, but they are captives and resent it."

Harry was allowed to accompany me to the strong wrought steel door which cut rational from irrational. His clammy, ghastly hands were placed one above and one below my hand.

"Come again, come soon. Ask these people to write to me, or to come see me." From his pocket he produced a list of names he had got from his daily newspaper—anybody's name. Some he may have heard of in some way, others were strangers. "It looks well in this place to have letters and visitors," he said to me behind the keeper's back. I took the list as I had taken other lists.

The next time I went to see him he would say, "Strange, they did not write, did not come."

"Too bad! but you see, people are very busy these days."

"I suppose so," he sighed. "Ask at the office as you go out if I can get out of here to spend Christmas with you."

I went through the iron door. The keeper clapped it shut quickly. I went out of the building. How beautiful the free world looked!

The worst visit I had with Harry was the week after my sister's death. He had read of it in his paper. Harry met me at the dividing door. A keeper was with him.

The keeper said, "I am afraid, Miss, the visitor's room is busy today—Board meeting—this way please."

We climbed two long flights of caged stairs and passed down bare grim corridors with open doors leading into stark sleeping wards. Bed, pillow, chair; bed, pillow, chair; bed, pillow, chair, down both walls of the long straight rooms; that was all each man's allotment. They were spotlessly clean and neatly made, those beds. A centre aisle ran from door to barred window. "You can go in here and sit to chat," said the keeper, drawing two of the wooden chairs side by side. While turning round I contrived to kick the chairs further apart. The guard began his pacing up and down outside in the corridor. They never left a patient unguarded. Each time he passed the door he looked in.

"I am dreadfully sorry about your sister," Harry began and sprang from his chair. He was club-footed and his amble was slow.

Good Heavens, was he going to kiss his sympathy! His loose lips and prickly whiskered cheeks, his dull eyes and scarred forehead were almost . . . The keeper! Oh, thank Heaven!

Harry was back in his seat in a jiffy. He waited till the man had turned and re-passed the door. This end of the corridor was the longer, he would be back not quite so quickly. I saw Harry edging towards me. He sprang clumsily. I had pushed my chair till it was close beside the open door. Harry pulled up his chair. "I'm sorry . . ."

The guard did not go the full length but doubled back. He made some trivial remark to me. Again Harry bounced back into his seat when the guard was in sight. He waited four passings of the man. I talked of all the little trivial happenings I thought would interest him; his replies were more vacant than usual. The keeper reassured, resumed his beat the whole length of the corridor.

Harry bent over me, his claw-like hand on my shoulder. I wriggled from under his hand. If that dreadful mouth touched my cheek I would yell. I jumped into the doorway, called, "Guard, please tell me the time. I must catch the early bus today. I am sorry Harry that I am not able to stay today."

He slunk back to his seat, discouraged. He said, "I have not half told you how sorry I am about your sister."

"Never mind, I know you are. Good-bye."

He said, "I wanted to tell you about my new job, too. They let me polish the brass spittoons. Everybody can't be trusted. The polish is poison and they drink it. Polishing brass is a trust!"

"I'm so glad they have given you a trust job."

"Come to our concert," Harry begged. "We have a good band among the patients, and besides that, musicians come from town to help."

My sister and I went. Harry was allowed to sit with us in the seats reserved for visitors. The patients were massed in the centre part of the hall. Harry told us in great whispers their names and what they had been before they came here. Some were sulky, some jovial, some meek, some fierce. "Only the well ones are allowed to come to concerts. There are lots more upstairs, 'bad ones,'" volunteered Harry. From those present one judged the "bad ones." The concert went very well till it neared the end, then above the wail of the fiddles, the banging of the drum, the squeals of the flutes rose the terrifying whistling screech of epilepsy.

The epileptic was in the very centre of the lunatics. Incredibly fast, six keepers were upon him. They lifted him, rigid as a board, over the heads of the sitting men and carried him out a side door. The lunatics took no notice, the music played right on.

"It is nothing," whispered Harry. "He has five or six of those a day, they don't hurt and when he wakes up he remembers nothing about them."

"God save the King!" Everybody stood, and great mugs of hot coffee and hunks of cake were brought to the patients, who came back and back for more; apparently there was no stint.

Supper was to be served in the Superintendent's room, for visitors. We did not wait. It was good to be out in fresh air and sanity again.

THE POLICEMAN'S RETALIATION

Edna, the farm girl called in to chaperone me at the missionaries'
and I had trudged three miles in dust and heat; so it was good, when
we got there, to see the little green patch that was White Skidegate. It
had a wharf, a whale-oil refinery, a muddle of cabins and a hotel. All
except the oil refinery were huddled into a little cleared patch of green
grass, surrounded by sombre fir forests climbing up low hills on
a never-ending slope. Beyond those rolling tree-clad hills came
what? What did the "beyond" lead to? Perhaps it was better not to
think. One only got perplexed and muddled thinking about the vast-
ness of the land.

Mrs. Fraser was in her lean-to kitchen at the hotel. Mail days
were always busy, but Sunday mail days were extra busy. Settlers
in boats might come from anywhere at any hour and want meals.
There was always a slim chance that there might be mail for them.
The mail boat was due any time between midnight Sunday and the
noon of Monday.

There were few women and no children about White Skidegate.
Bachelors there were in plenty, greedy for Mrs. Fraser's cookery
after their own haphazard messes. Missionaries told of calling on

one bachelor and being given bread to eat in which Keating's insect powder[1] had been used in mistake for baking powder. Mrs. Fraser onioned lavishly. You could smell her onions clear round the bend of the road on the cliff.

"Can you put us up for the night, Mrs. Fraser?" I asked.

"Surely." She lifted a lid and stirred something savoury that interested her far more than we did.

She was too busy to show us our rooms, so we went to the wharf and sat ourselves on oil-barrels to rest. I said, "I prefer the smell of onions to oil, Edna." Eeither perfume was acceptable to Edna, saturated as she was with sea breezes and pine woods, pure nature smells. Onions and oil meant civilization, people, life.

The Missionary from the Indian village held an eventful service in the dining room after supper. Still Mrs. Fraser had not shown us where we were to sleep and we nodded with weariness.

"Let's turn in, that boat may cut our night short, end it any time after midnight."

Edna agreed, reluctantly. The Fraser Hotel was hilarity after the lighthouse seclusion of her own home.

"Show us our room please, Mrs. Fraser."

Mrs. Fraser's brows knit. "Let me see, now! I have not thought about that, in fact I have not got one. Every corner is full. There are only two bedrooms in the hotel. The cabins out on the green are every one bursting full." Her face beamed suddenly. "Why I have it—the policeman is away—you shall have his room."

She led us round the corner of the hotel to a cabin bigger than the rest. It had five beds, four were for the accommodation of villains

1. Keating's Persian Insect Destroying Powder *was manufactured by Thos. Keating, Chemist, in London. It was advertised to be effective against bedbugs, lice, fleas and other frequent visitors to logging camps and even respectable homes and establishments.*

and evildoers under police guard; the windows were barred. Every-thing was bare and unsmashable. Edna and I tumbled into two of the beds before Mrs. Fraser had turned to the door. "One moment, Mrs. Fraser," I shouted, "what about a key for our door?"

"A key? in Skidegate? Nobody locks doors." She hooked the chair (our only one) under the door knob. "Good Night."

I laid my clothes on the chair and crawled into the policeman's bed. My big sheepdog sprawled under my bed. Edna snored heav-ily as if she had been a villain weighty with wickedness. The night swallowed us all. We slept peacefully as birds on a tree top. Till— Between 1 and 2 a.m. I was startled by my dog darting from under the bed, angrily growling and barking. I was upright in a minute. There at the doorway was a man furiously wrestling with the chair.

"Who are you? Get out and shut that door!"

"I'm the Policeman, this is my room, get out yourself." The Po-liceman's voice was angry and had a drawl of deep weariness.

"Mrs. Fraser has rented this room to me for the night. I will set my dog on you if you don't go." I felt sorry for the man, but he could sleep better in his boat bunk than I could on an oil barrel.

"Mrs. Fraser had no right to rent my room, I'm dead beat," he yawned. "This is my room. It's my room," he repeated doggedly.

"For tonight it is rented to me. Please, please, go away, I am so tired." I felt my voice quivering in my throat like jelly. It was hard on us both. I don't know where his work had taken him; mine had led me through discomfort and hard travel for many days.

The dog came into the patch of moonlight, showed his bulk and aired his growl.

He said spitefully, "Whoever you are, woman or girl, serve you right if I turned you out." With a final jerk the man wrenched and worked the chair from under the door knob. It flew on its side, then the door banged. We heard him go from cabin to cabin, pounding on doors rattling knobs, begging admittance.

Edna was stuffing the pillow into her mouth to strangle her giggles. "I know that policeman," she said. "He is a nice man, very shy. He'd never have turned us out."

At last the pounding, barking, giggling that had cracked Skidegate's silence, mended. Night knit itself serenely together again. I felt sorry for the policeman till the next morning. After that, he could have slept standing on his head on an oil barrel for all I cared. I hoped he had been uncomfortable.

"Edna, Edna! Where are my clothes?" There was not a stitch in the room except the night-gown I stood in. Edna's clothes were on her now; they had been on the foot of her bed. Mine had been on the chair.

"Look outside," suggested Edna.

There they sprawled, dew-bedraggled and exposed, in the direct pathway of Skidegate's scant population and of the visitors waiting for the steamer. All had seen them when they went to the hotel for breakfast; they had all trampled over them. The wind had spread them like a window-display, corsets and bustle as centrepiece. It was the day of bustle fashion; mine was a wire contraption—perhaps the men thought I carried a patent rat trap with me.

I did not go to breakfast till the oil-refinery whistle blew. The steamer came shortly after. I strode straight from hotel to boat, looking neither to right or to left. If the policeman was anywhere about I did not see him.

Note: *The "eventful service in the dining room after supper," with Brother Gow's prayer took place on this same day. See "Prayers and Pickles" (p. 137).*

SOME FREEDOM, SOME RELIGION

Three years and a half in San Francisco at the Art school had loosened the clamp that pressed upon and tried to keep me down at home. Loosening but not entirely freeing me. My art teaching earned me money—freedom more or less—and the old barn studio provided a corner that was all my own. Then, too, I owned a dog, something I had wanted all my life. Of course the dog had to be walked. He was not allowed in the house or the garden. When he was not actually with me, he was ordered chained. The necessity to take the dog for walks meant that I had the freedom of the gates and came and went without having to explain myself.

Through Walt Whitman I learned that the beaches were mine, the woods were mine, all Beacon Hill was mine. And the woods, to go to them alone or with my pupils was part of my work. So the family considered it quite permissible, and I realized the full joy of Whitman's wisdom when he said:

To see no possession, but you may possess it, enjoying all without labour or purchase, abstracting the feast yet not abstracting one particle of it.[1]

1. From Walt Whitman's poem "Song of the Open Road", section 13.

Was not that exactly what I was doing?

Our home was crammed to the ceiling with religious activities. The Elder and Bigger tried to snare me into good works, but beyond sometimes going to ordinary morning service with them, I kept aloof.

Bigger shooed good works towards me. The Elder tried to insist but her days of making me obey were over; when she tried to force I turned dumb as a plate. She said, "It would be a great comfort to me, Small, if you would be more cooperative in good works," but still I kept aloof. The house was swamped with religion. I believed in religion, but I was not in sympathy with the kind of religion ensconced in my own home.

I wanted to investigate others. I nibbled at this and at that. I had known something of Presbyterianism as a child. I tried the Christ Church Cathedral which was High Church and which our Bishop called popish; it was so terribly English. I tried several of the United Churches. I tried the Christian Science, and shyly the edges of the Roman Catholic, the Theosophy, and New Thought. Coming back where I started, I stood still.

One that appealed to me more than the rest was the service conducted by an up-and-doing Preacher who conducted services in the Royal Victoria Theatre, because he could get no other building big enough to accommodate the enormous following he had. I do not know what sect he called himself; it went by the name of Dr. Davies' Ministry.[1]

---

1. Clem Davies *born in England in 1890. He moved to Victoria in 1922 and set up a radio evangelical ministry. He relocated to Vancouver in 1937.*

He spoke clearly and he thought clearly, this man. I never heard anyone read the bible so understandingly or beautifully, pausing at some hard-to-comprehend verse and giving an explanation. They were not very conventional services but happy, uplifting services. People said malicious things about the man's private life; maybe they were true, maybe not. I did not care or think it any of my business. I sat in the dark quiet circular pit of the theatre and got something from what this man said. There was deep attentive silence while he preached. A great many stayed for the communion. It was very holy.

One Sunday morning the communion service was on a table close to the stage where the Preacher preached. The stage was well-lighted, but the pit was semi-lit. I sat close up for not hearing well. Suddenly, in the tense silence, I heard a tiny rustle, saw a vague movement. Two rats had come from somewhere and were sitting on their haunches, noses in the air smelling the communion bread. Horror filled me. I flung a hymn book over the front pew. The rats scuttled off and the congregation probably thought me a ruffian; nobody but me could see into the shadow under the table.

Dr. Davies' sermons were short. I got out earlier than the Reformed Episcopal Church that my sisters went to. I passed the Empress Hotel on the way home and walked through the lounge into their beautiful conservatory, concluding my Sunday morning worship among the flowers. There were seats about and the displays of flowers were superb. There was the humid hot earth smell of pampered growth, there was a tinkling fountain under the high glass dome. The high dome exaggerated the trickle noise; in reality it was only a drip. The fountain's tiles were hideous and in reality it was no bigger than a bath tub. But, turn your back, shut your eyes, it was quite lovely among all the other delights of the conservatory.

The Elder and Bigger lived in the old home. Middle came from her house and Small from hers, and we all dined together on Sunday in the old home. Small was the only one of the family to stray from the Church they were brought up in.

One day I went to the Theatre as usual. I had been away for some weeks, visiting. The doors stood open but there was no one in the vestibule. I went in and opened the inner swing doors. The pit was all velvety darkness. Chilled, I came away. After gathering an immense congregation together, the Preacher had gone to Vancouver to accumulate larger congregations still. In Vancouver he filled an immense arena; then he tired even of that success and went to California in search of yet greater fields. We felt let down. I stood pondering and for a while went nowhere.

THE ROUND WORLD

Gerhard rang me up on a Sunday afternoon. The broad foreign accent was very pronounced. "Mees Emilie Carr? I bring to you greetings from Mees Kathrine Dreier,[1] artist of New York! My friend and I make tour of your country. We tire of New York and wish to see something of Canada, my friend Klaus and I. He is engineer, me I am modern architect. I should like to call at your studio and see your picture. Yes? We have travel now for three month. We buy old candy delivery car and fix her up with bunk. We can go where we want to go."

I said, "I will be pleased to receive you in my studio," and they came.

It was years since World War I was over, yet feeling was still bitter against Germany. But when the two boys presented themselves, who could feel bitterness against these young fresh-faced boys in their twenties? I figured they would have been too young to be in the war. Then I forgot war and boundaries and enjoyed the men. They told me they were staying two days for themselves. "Only two days in Victoria." They were going up-Island next day. One was an artist, one an architect. They had been living in New York two years,

1. Katherine Dreier (1877-1952) was a painter, patron, writer and promoter of modern art; Emily met her in New York City in 1930.

were now out to see the continent of North America.

The German boys had travelled most intelligently. I enjoyed their experiences. When Gerhard began to talk about modern architecture I was absorbed. His enthusiasm in his work was delightful. He drew little designs to explain the modern viewpoint. We had a pleasant afternoon.

They were keen on going north, spending a winter in Alaska. I offered to take them to call on a yacht whose skipper, an author, had travelled in the north country extensively. The yacht lay in a bay some miles out of town. They postponed their up-Island trip so as to go. We drove out in the boys' car and spent a very pleasant hour or two on the yacht. The day following, the boys went up-Island.

Four days later they came back to Victoria, so charmed with the surroundings that they had decided to stay a fortnight on our Island. During their up-Island trip, a very English old lady had come to stay with me. I was putting supper on the table when the boys telephoned. "We come back! Your country is beautiful."

"Come out and have a bite," I said, "We are just going to sit down to table." They accepted.

I said to the old lady, "I will delay supper a few minutes; I have guests, two German boys."

The old lady stuck out all her prickles and "Ahem!"ed fifteen times; she went on knitting with pursed lips. "If my daughter Lena was here," she volunteered presently, "she would get up and walk out of your house!"

"She would be welcome to," I retorted. I could see the old lady intended to be nasty to the boys.

Gerhard brought me a big bunch of red roses and offered them with the courteous deference befitting my years. He had told me I made him think of his mother. He loved nature, this boy, and seemed hungry to talk of his mother and his cabin in the Black Forest and of everything beautiful in Art and Nature.

During the meal the old lady thawed. The lads treated her with grandmotherly deference, which pleased her. After supper a young man from next door came in, also my very straight-laced religious sister. We spent a delightful evening—mention of the War was carefully avoided. Our little world seemed to expand. The Germans had been several years in New York. They knew a lot, yet were not aggressively informative. They were very keen on my painting and asked me to show pictures, which I did. The old lady despised my painting, so did my sister. My work since I had returned from the Paris Art Schools did not please Victorians, but the boys understood what I was trying for. I felt lifted about my work-problems while talking to them. The others listened to the newer viewpoint in painting and to Gerhard's new architectural schemes with bored amusement.

One day during their stay, the boys took me for an all-day picnic in their car. We took a picnic lunch and ate it in the woods on top of a high bluff on the Malahat Drive. We had discussed Walt Whitman together in the studio. I took *Leaves of Grass* along and read aloud after lunch. I read "Song of the Rolling Earth" and it seemed just the place and just the company to make every word ring true. When the long day ended we went home happy and peaceful in our hearts. I thought, "Oh world, you are very round. Your ends meet perfect as a ring. You are soft and harmless as a baby's woolly ball," then I went to sleep.

I invited a few young people into the Studio one evening to meet the German boys. There was interesting general conversation and I showed pictures. Every one of those guests came to me afterwards and said how glad they were I had invited them. They said it made them realize something deeper about the world that they had been missing. They felt the world smaller and themselves bigger and like myself, they had felt the encircling roundness.

After they left Victoria the German boys drove down to California then out into the desert of Arizona. From there they wrote me interesting letters. The desert had been a wonderful experience for them. They spent Christmas there. Gerhard wrote, "I know of nowhere I would rather be for Christmas than at your Studio, unless it be my mother's home in Germany." They sent me a little box of small out-of-the-way bits of nothings, desert flowers pressed, twigs of this and that, and the warmest greetings. Then, a long, long pause, no letters came from the German boys.

The next I heard was from Gerhard in Russia. "My friend became ill in the desert, pneumonia. I took him to hospital in Los Angeles. He died. I sold the car. I had hardly courage to go on alone, but I did. I went to Russia. The Russians are wonderful people. They make of their country a great country. Some day I shall go back there. I am at my mother's now very ill. I am glad we made the trip. The roundness of the world is true! and the ends meet."

I answered his letter and sent him a sketch, one of my big woods ones. He wrote, "It delights me. It hangs at the foot of my bed and I am back in your great western forests." I heard several times after that. He wrote well with quaint phrasing. He was designing model towns and happy, his heart in his work.

War—Silence.

I could never look on those boys as enemies. I could never feel them German and me as Canadian, their enemy. I could only feel their nation and mine were slivers of the same world because of that love of nature which we shared. I could not feel race when talking with them. We were People and the world was round. There were no seams in her. She was all of a piece.

MONKEYS AND THE DARK

When young, dark was to me a dreadful thing; to have it all around squeezing was fearful. Up to the time of the monkey episode I do not remember fear of the dark.

The monkey episode took place when I was a child of perhaps five or six. We were tucked in bed. Our room was at the head of the stairs. There was a mad pealing of the front doorbell. It was unusual in our quiet home for the bell to ring this late, 9:30 in the evening. My father and mother came out of the door on one side of the hall, my big sister and her fiancé came out of the door on the other side. Between them they opened the front door. Two shrill treble voices, a boy's and a girl's, high with fear and excitement squealed, "Come, oh, please come quickly, it's a monkey and it's biting our little boys and Father and Mother are out!"

My pretty sister and her fiancé went out into the night with the children. The cold air stopped rushing up the stairs when the door shut. We were out of bed in our nighties. The children's excitement had caught us.

"Go back to bed," said Mother. "It is nothing."

"The children said it was a monkey," said Middle. "Gracious, I'm scared!"

In bed Middle gave a comfortable grunt and turned into her pillow to sleep. When Father and Mother came upstairs I was still wide awake. My sister and her fiancé came back and called up to them.

"They have sent for the owner of the beast. It was unmanageable and the children are bitten and terrified."

The elders were all very indignant about the loose monkey. What had happened was this. These, our nearest neighbours, lived in a house set back in a large treed garden. Having put their six children to bed, the couple went out for a walk. The oldest girl heard the door open. She called, "Is that you , Mother?" There was no answer, only a rush of cold wind from the open door. The girl went back to bed. As she did so, a furry something brushed her bare foot. Thinking it was the cat, the girl paid no heed and was nearly asleep when sounds of cries and animal snarls came from the room where two small boys slept. The girl rushed in, calling to a bigger brother. A fairly large animal was bouncing up and down on the bed gibbering angrily while the small boys fought it in their sleep. The big children stood paralysed, not knowing what to do. If they approached the bed, the monkey bared her teeth and made gruesome faces.

"Go for the Carrs," said the boy.

"I'm afraid of the dark," said the girl.

"Then I'll go and you stay,"

"I'll be afraid of the monkey if I stay."

So they both went barefoot and in their nightgowns. The little boys were quite badly bitten by the monkey. While they were away the monkey was excited; even the woman who owned her had difficulty in catching her.

The police made the woman get rid of the big monkey but she got two small ones in its place. She kept the old Colonist Hotel and said the antics of her monkeys brought trade. She did not keep her monkeys caged or chained; they often strayed into our fields, and I am now ashamed to remember how terrified I was of the creatures.

Those were the first monkeys I had ever seen and in some way I got them associated with the devil. I gave to them supernatural powers. They had hands and could open doors. What else could they do? My life was an agony of fear which I was ashamed to tell anyone. The dark and monkeys were synonymous, were all jumbled into one horror in my mind. When I got into bed at night my feet could not be driven to go down into the bed, there might be a monkey down there. I looped myself so that head and feet were both on my pillow and I was ashamed to tell anyone, not even Middle. Only she and I knew the reason.

It was not till I grew up that I forced myself to go into a pet shop if there was a monkey. It was not till I went to London and strong-minded Mrs. Radcliffe took me to the London Zoo, and I could not face her derision, that I forced myself to stand beside her in the monkey house and give the monkeys stare for stare and let them stroke my hand.

By now I had disassociated monkeys and the devil; dark and monkeys were still one to me. I had an Art School sketching ticket that permitted me to go to the London Zoo as often as I wished. I went often and each time I forced myself into the monkey house. First I got used to them, then I got to be amused, then I liked them, then I loved; eventually I owned a monkey. When my fear of monkeys went, my fear of the dark went too.

My eyes always seem to open much wider in the dark than in the light. We were a sizeable family and I was seldom left alone after night fell. If I was, I opened all the doors and windows and went into the garden and sang. It always seemed to me nothing much could happen to one who was singing.

BECKLEY STREET

The movers were finished and gone, the door of the dishevelled cottage was shut, the mess and uprooting of the move was all about me. For a month I had toiled without help, cleaning and sorting, picking over, selling, condemning as garbage. I had sold my four-suite apartment house. The buyer wanted possession immediately. I said, "I will put every effort into leaving my old place nice." The cottage I was moving into I was renting. I could settle it at my leisure. Here I was, in, but too dog-tired to move a finger, sitting on a wooden stool just inside the cottage door, crying timidly, crying for very tiredness. Here the good angel Willie found me and was as stunned by embarrassment as I was shamed by my tears.

"Seems to me you need some help," said Willie, eyeing the mountains of muddle. He had wonderful furniture power and began pushing into place, lighting fires, hanging pictures, assembling head, foot, sides and mattress of my bed, calming the monkey, hushing the dog and teasing me into smiles. Willie the good, always out to help lame dogs over styles.

There is in most women a joyousness that bubbles up from her depths when she starts setting up a home. It is a trait that belongs to the feminine, be it broody hen, mother cat or a human lady. It is the innate love for fixing herself a nest. Sometimes when I remember all the crude deplorable camps I have coaxed not only into livableness, but into lovableness as well, then I know surely that I am a woman, a homemaker. It was born in me.

Beckley Street lay in a working man's district. My sister Bigger was shocked that I should go there to live. "It is not the Carr's environment and setting," said Bigger and pursed her lips in disapproval.

Middle shrugged. "It is certainly not the district I would choose. I suppose it is quite respectable and your own business, but is not what Carrs are used to."

First and foremost, the old-fashioned cottage had high windows and plenty of light which was essential for my painting. That to my sisters was of minor importance. They did not recognize painting as my very life.

Beckley Street was only one block long and blind at both ends, yet soon I had more friends up and down Beckley Street than I had all round the four sides of the block on Simcoe Street. They were simple people, many of them on relief. As artist, I was an enigma to them. If they came to see me they kept their eyes averted from the walls in disapproval. I entertained them anywhere in the house rather than in my studio, so as to save them and me embarrassment. It was the same when my sisters came to see me. They always made me feel as if my painting was indecent. It was not, unless you call the endeavour to bore into the heart of nature, or trying to probe instead of being satisfied with skin-deep surfaces, indecent.

The children of Beckley Street amused me immensely. Their games were largely self-invented. I watched their play from behind my curtains. I did not want to spoil their delightful un-self-consciousness.

Our houses had narrow strips of garden between them. The family on one side of me had one little girl and several big brothers. The family on the other side had two small girls. The three little girls played together on a strip of green on one side of me, or in a planked back yard on the other, according to the type of game they were playing. Sometimes they staged entertainment where each child did part of the programme, one a dance, one a song.

Other times they played "costumers." A pile of miscellaneous rags were heaped in a corner. The purchasing lady was loaded with rags: head, shoulders, waist and always a train draggling behind. Sometimes there were two purchasers to one seller, sometimes two sellers to one purchaser. The seller, after draping the rags on the purchaser, would stand back, wring her hands and roll her eyes exclaiming, "So becoming, Modame, so tremendously becoming! But let me show you this mantle Modame, just the thing for the Opera!"

One day I was working in my garden when a small voice piped across the fence.

"Any milk today, Mum? We have a cow farm now."

"Half a pint of milk and a quart of rich cream," I ordered.

"I'll tell the milkmaid." And, turning to the small girl sitting on the back door step, she shouted, "Jane, milk the best cow, at once."

"Which is the best?"

"'Cream cow', the Jersey of course, top step."

Jane came with a beer bottle filled with water and a tomato can. She sat on the top step and slowly poured from the bottle into the can, drop by drop.

"Is the top cow the cream cow, too, Ma'am?"

"Of course, stupid! Every step is a cow. Of course, the top step is the cream cow."

I discovered each step represented a higher grade cow; the higher the step, the better the grade.

There were boating parties too on the vacant lot opposite my home. Little girls in apple boxes with regiments of dolls tucked in beside them would row furiously. The boats did a lot of tipping but made no progress. Finally they turned over and there were cries of, "Help! I drown! I drown!" The lady and her children were rescued from the parched grass billows, the doll rubbed down and given imaginary hot drinks from old cans salvaged from rubbish dumps. I could work myself into as keen a rescuer as any by just watching from my window.

I was very happy in Beckley Street.

There was an old German woman aged ninety-five, living in Beckley Street. In spite of the creak and groaning of her years, she was wonderfully spry. She was poor but not eligible for city relief, though she had done charring in Victoria ever since she was a young woman. Because her husband had never taken out naturalization papers, now she was not eligible. He had been dead many years. Her family had married poor men and drifted away to the States, all but one daughter who was on relief.

The old woman held a reception in her cottage on her birthday. She notified all her former char clients of the approaching date afresh each year, and they came to see her and stocked her cupboard well.

Some benevolent society or other made her a very small allowance. She owned her cottage and was excused taxes by the City. She chopped her own wood and grew her own potatoes. If you took her anything she always paid back. The next day, along would come a grandchild with a monster potato of her own growing, or an apron made by her bony old fingers, cut from impossible patterns and the stitches were so long they caught on everything.

On her ninety-sixth birthday, a young reporter came hunting copy. She was out painting her fence, while her daughters that had come from the States to celebrate with her stood watching.

"Ugh!" said the woman, addressing the reporter and waving her hand in the direction of her daughters. "Ach! girls of now time dey aint no good for strong! Me, I paint my fence an' me ninety-six! Them girls is only seventy-two an' seventy-five, dey most too tired to put eats in dey's moufs."

The last time I went to see her I thought Grannie would not paint fences much longer.

"I don' know what the matter of me. Befo' I scrup ceiling every year, this year no, climb so—" Like a shot she had mounted her trembling old self onto a chair. "Me go so," she swung her arms as if scrubbing above her head. "Round, round, round, he all go black for me. I don' know what matter of me."

Some charitable busy bodies insisted that she be taken to hospital. Away from the seclusion of her own cottage, the hospital ward sent her frantic. She made such commotion they had to bring her home to die.

The last year I was in Beckley Street, the ramshackle duplex opposite my cottage, where the drains were always being torn up and the tenants moved every few months, housed a family on relief. The husband was a ne'er-do-well, the wife a disheartened woman with one toddling child. What did they do but go and have twins! With nothing to clothe even one babe in.

The Beckley Street ladies assembled in my cottage. We made a social sewing bee of it, equipping the twins from the toes up; ran up two layettes, while drinking tea. All the ladies in Beckley Street that I knew came. It was my farewell to them; the cottage had been sold. I was moving.

Good-bye Beckley Street. I loved you and am glad I lived in and was taught by you.

HEAD OF THE FAMILY

I am sure our childhood could not have comprehended any human, a more Almighty being on earth, than was my Father. His word was absolute. He was stern but we reverenced him more for that.

Father told us that God had appointed man three score years and ten to live on this earth, and he himself died punctually at seventy. I think he would have considered it like giving God back-chat to have overstepped his time limit. Mother predeceased Father by two years. He did his best to keep her longer, but she died at the age of fifty. Twenty years was between their ages at his death. Father was eighteen years older than Mother to start with, so that within two years our house was left without a head.

The "Elder," my oldest sister, immediately stepped into Father's shoes. Father had been forced to be tender with his feet because of his gout. The Elder's step was hard firm. The Elder's rule was more acute even than Father's. She was always at home, and now there was no intervening Mother to appeal to. My sister strove with us because she loved to dominate.

Father's fierce rule had the determination behind it of bringing his family up right. Occasionally I had seen him with a slight scowl overlook some small naughtiness, as when Dick rushed to the dinner table almost late and hurried his hands under the cloth.

"Did you wash your hands before coming to table?"

"Yes, Father."

Now, we could see, and so could Father, that the palms only had come in contact with soap. The backs were very grubby. Had that been the Elder, Dick would have been due a touch of riding whip around his black-stockinged legs. Father went on eating, ignoring the almost-lie.

Dick's and my black stockings were well-acquainted with that riding whip. Bigger and Middle never got it. It would have been no fun whipping Bigger. She would have taken it as "chastening from the Lord" and the Elder would not have liked the Lord to take the credit for her chastisements. Middle's path was the way of least resistance. She went her own way and pretended she was going the Elder's. So Dick and I took the family whackings till Dick was sent to Ridley College in the East.

I had never "Eldered" Dick in spite of my four year's seniority. He was a delicate little fellow. He contracted T.B. in the East and was advised to go down south. He went to Santa Barbara and died there some years later; then I was the youngest of the family without argue.

The Elder wore Father's stern shoes as if she had been born in them. We were such little steps, Bigger, Middle and I. It seemed we were a bunch of contemporaries with neither head nor tail. We were middle-aged women when, in her sixty-ninth year, the Elder died. In family affairs, Bigger had always been fussy but meek; when it came to big things, she was determined. The Elder and Bigger had lived on together in the old home and Bigger was completely dominated by the Elder. It was amazing to see her evolve, magnify herself and take place as head of the family after the Elder's death.

She was good at business and pulled the place up, got after mending and back taxes the Elder had let drift. Middle and I went to her for advice in business problems. She loved being consulted and her advice was good, though we usually asked but went our own way. Bigger ruled very much as the eldest Miss Carr. Then she too died and that wretched little nigger rhyme would buzz in my head: "Ten little nigger boys . . . " and now we were down to two. I had never thought of a family of two having a head and a tail but apparently it does.

We went down to the undertaking parlours to take things for Bigger. The head of the establishment was engaged. We were put in the office to wait. A falsely blond girl was at the counter violently lipsticked. A cheeky loud-voiced man breezed in and lolling across the counter tickled the powder off her nose with a flower and made coarse jokes. A boy was mopping down the front hall singing, of all things, "Ten little nigger boys." Beyond, we could hear the organ wheezing out a hymn, accompanied by sniffles; there was a funeral in progress.

"Come! I can't bear any more! We will go into the waiting room. Perhaps it will be quieter there." I bounced off but it was worse there. The nigger boy song was at the door. The walls were hung with photos of gravestones and models of more were on the shelf. There was a black carpet with a grey border, a wicker lounge and two chairs that groaned and creaked. There was a roll-top desk and on it were files and files of funeral bills, great cruel bills extorting people for splurge funerals while wanting for their dead dignified simplicity instead of show-off.

I was all riled up and Middle was annoyed with me. She said, "You ought to calm yourself," and showed her own superior self-control by caressing a model tombstone on the desk.

"Don't you bring me here to be buried!" I flared. "Don't you!"

"Don't you take me anywhere else," she retorted. "They go to our church and they have always buried our dead."

"They've buried themselves too. These are only successors. It's a beastly place. No quiet, no dignity."

"Miss Carr?" The head was in the door. I don't know how much he had heard, nor do I care.

Middle stepped forward, "I am Miss Carr." But Middle hated making arrangements of all sorts. She handed the parcel over to me. Suddenly it occurred to me I did not know how to ask for my dead sister. Middle had said "I am Miss Carr." I jumbled a "late" into the sentence somewhere. The man took Bigger's dainty gown from the parcel and strained it through fingers coarse as a bunch of sausages.

"It'll do," he said. "She ain't fixed yet. Won't take a jiffy. I'll call when she's ready, that door." Pointing, he was gone. He only wanted a white apron and a knife to turn him into a complete butcher.

"Ready," he shouted down the hall as if Bigger was there waiting to play a game of hide and seek with us.

"Don't you bring me!"

Then we were in the tiny room with only Bigger's coffin in it for furniture. Flowers were beginning to come, a soft shaded light was on her face, a face utterly serene, all the fret and worry wrinkles habitual to her in life were gone. My fret and fidgets had gone too. We looked and came quietly home.

There were letters in my cottage post box. I took them out and automatically slipped my finger under the flaps. Middle stretched out a hand.

"Miss Carr, I think! Remember from now, I am Miss Carr. You are Miss Emily. You can never be the oldest, the family head. You were and will be tail, always, even should I die first."

LISPING

From a finishing school in England, a girl came home to her father and brother and sister in Victoria. The girl's mother had died when she was born. We knew the family well and my mother was fond of the little girl, or young lady as she had become. She was very pretty. Everyone petted her. It was the only thing that made me jealous, when I saw my mother pet an outside little girl. I was not jealous of my own sisters but I could not bear to see her pet girl children that were not her own. I did not mind her petting small boys because I knew three of hers had died.

My father and mother were particular over our speech. No affectations, no fancy mannerisms and above all no slang was allowed in our house. This little girl had acquired an affected lisp while abroad. She was several years older than I, and little girls love to copy big ones. I tried to copy the lisp, thinking that if Mother liked this child so well, perhaps she'd like me better with a lisp.

Mother detected the affectation at once. "Why must you pick up the only silly affectation that girl has brought back with her? It is not natural for her to lisp. By and by she will drop it. Her head has been a little turned, poor child. She has no mother. But you, please, you will stop it right now."

I was terribly ashamed that Mother had seen through me. I shooed the lisp from my tongue.

That summer I went to stay at the seaside with my best friend. She was one of a big family whose father and mother thought they were marvellous. The eldest boy lisped. His mother encouraged it, thinking it cute. I was aware then how stupid it was and grateful to Mother for having shamed me out of the habit.

I went through life to the age of seventy quite normal in speech. Then I had to have my teeth pulled and replaced by false plates. The uppers were all right. After a year or two passed, the lowers had to be drawn and substituted.

Finally I went into town for the final fitting of my lower teeth. The dentist put my lowers in and asked, "Do they feel comfortable?"

"No," I replied and got into the taxi unhappy about the jaw.

When I got home and began to talk, I discovered to my disgust that I was lisping. A lisp, firmly twisted in among my lower teeth. I could not spit it out.

Everybody pretended not to notice because they saw I was so mad, but I'm sure they were aware of it. I said, "I could bite that dentist!" Those who knew me nodded comprehendingly.

THE WAGGING FINGER

"Don't do it, I can't bear it! I'll screech, I'll tear your wagging finger off!"

I was little when you found out how it enraged me, to set a wagging forefinger in my face and be told that it served me right and such and such were my desserts. You made me see red and I wanted to be wicked. It makes me just as mad in my seventieth year. Father and Mother never did it. Just Bigger and the Elder did.

I preferred the whip to that wagging finger. My big sister loved us, I know, but her way of loving was hard. When I think of my sister now, and she has been dead over 20 years, it is not her face I see, but that wagging index finger. Why did she waggle that at me, when she knew how I hated it? And it made me ugly, oh why?

When I stood by her coffin, looking down at her still face, I felt suddenly that long forefinger beating the air, for all it lay so still across her, and I bent and drew the flowers up a little to hide the index finger.

Note: *This story is about her oldest sister* Edith *(the Elder); she was born in 1856 and died in 1919.*

GRINNING

I detest people who continually grin. No need to perpetually scowl or to cry, but why perpetually grin? A set grin that the modern photographer insists on these days, the old photographers would have scorned to perpetuate and to photograph. They did not expect grins, seeing you were held rigid with the aid of an iron rod down your spine with a forked iron headrest at the top. There you were, fixed for as many minutes as he counted on the watch in his hand.

To be sure, dentistry had not made such strides in those days, and people were not so anxious to show all the money they had put into their mouths in gold. The modern photograph often looks more like a cross between a dentist's showcase and a fleshless skull, with the pose of an actress thrown in to make it look like a human.

Photographed faces are wearisome things, but if they wear an everlasting grin as well, they are horrible and insincere. Look through the old family album. The clothing is often outlandish, the hair like nature grew it, dress, astounding! The studio setting is conventional, but the people in those photographs have a dignified restraint which the grinning photographs of today never attain. The photo-makers (who now call themselves Artists) favour vapid theatrical poses, nothing human behind the grin.

There is the pitiful grin; it is the grin of fear. One sees it on the faces of monkeys and dogs when they do not understand cruelty. A self protective showing of the teeth . . . a warning.

The beautiful faces of flowers never suggest a grin. The steadfast purpose of the faces of animals in their natural setting is without the falseness of a grin they do not feel. Steady determination to fulfil their span of life and to perpetuate their kind: these are a creature's full expression. He does not have to grin, he expresses himself all over.

MOTHERING

There was a motherly woman. She married a widower with six children, and then by him she had a baby of her own. She was not very young when she married the widower, but she had not had any experience in rearing children. Sometimes she was afraid, and then she ran over to our house, which was across the corner, to ask Mother's advice. Their house was set far back in a deep wild garden.

One day, Mother sent me to this woman with a message. A young step-daughter answered my knock and said, "Mother is in the nursery, you had better come to her there," so I followed the girl.

The woman sat in a low rocking chair cuddling her baby on one arm. She held her other hand out to me in greeting, calling me some little feminine pet name and drew me close. I had never kissed this woman before but somehow I wanted to today, and I did. Suddenly I was shy and embarrassed and wondered why I had.

"You haven't seen my baby yet have you?" she said lifted the soft woolly shawl that lay across the baby and her shoulder. His head was big and round and downy. Then I saw that he was feeding. His greedy lips were clinging to his mother's white breast. I drew back abashed, for I had never seen a young child feed from his mother.

"Our baby is nice, isn't he," said the little step-girl.

"Very," I replied. Her face wasn't pink a bit like mine was.

For the first time I realized what a very real part babies were of their mothers. When I kissed that Mother Woman I do not think it was she alone I kissed but every mother in the world. I understood that mothers gave to their children their very life.

When our baby was born I was too young, except perhaps to feel a slight jealousy at my place being usurped. Later I occasionally saw a woman bare herself and feed her child in a public place with a feeling of embarrassment and disgust. These mothers never woke in me the still holy feeling that first feeding mother did. I am glad the first time I saw it everything was so beautiful.

BURNING THE BIBLES

An empty box stood in an empty room in an empty house. On each side of the box was a bare table. There was a fire in the room, one chair and a red rosewood piano. In front of the fire was a big pile of books on the floor. Two old women sat, one on the edge of the box, and one in the only chair of the room. The women were Middle and Small. They were both over seventy years old, and these were the very last things in Bigger's house, and they were clearing them away.

The books were all religious books. On top of the pile sat the immense family Bible. Middle lifted it with both hands and laid it on the little old rosewood piano where her hat and gloves lay.

"Mine," she said "Mine as the head of the family now."

"Of course," said Small.

Of everything in the dismantled house, it was the only thing she would have liked to have had, not exactly religiously. Small and her family had never seemed such a complete unit anywhere else as in the old family Bible. There were the brothers John, Thomas and William, who had died long before Small was born; and there were Mother, Father, Dick, Tallie and the Elder; and now there was Bigger, all among the dead. Tallie was the only one of them that marched through the three columns: birth, marriage, death.

"Begin, Small."

Small stooped and took a volume from the pile before Middle.

"Its four brothers are there too," Middle said, "All bound in calf."

"Saints are heavy, they had better go to the bottom of the box for the auction rooms."

"Pass them over, first all inscriptions on fly-leaves must be taken out."

There were sets and couplets, prayer and hymn books bound together, and there were presents and prize Sunday School books. Bible, Bible, Bibles, five of them in a row and every one requiring a microscopic or telescope to read. Gifts from the youth who have no compassion for failing sight.

There was an immense series of ready-made sermons. I'd heard most of them delivered from the Reformed Episcopal pulpit. Their parson had lived in my sister's suite when she bisected the old home—being too vast for Bigger alone. The sermons were in a little-used room and saved the parson time to go in and seize a ready-made.

One of the tables beside the auction boxes was entirely for religion straight, that is, Bibles, prayer books and hymnals. The other table was heaped with semi-religious mottoes for good behaviour and help for daily living. These were to go to Bigger's missionary friends as keepsakes.

"How shall we dispose of *Roman Catholicism Exposed* and *As it Was in the Beginning*," asked Small.

"Auction box!"

"What a prize for somebody, a whole crate of Religion all for fifty cents! Unless Middle, you'd like to add two bits and keep it?"

"Don't be infuriating, Small."

"Not in the least," said Small, taking a loose plank and spanking Josephus[1] into a tighter fit so as to nail the lid on.

The two women leant wearily back. "Only one thing more: the Bibles!"

You can't toss Bibles round to take chances.

"Come, Small, and bring the poker and an armful of those tiny-print Bibles."

Middle herself took the tongs, an armful of Israel Banners[2] and a box of matches.

The sisters crept stealthily as if in crime. Halfway down the wide gravel walk there was a little pile of white ashes, family fragments that could neither be taken or left. Middle raked the ashes together, a light pile of Banners on top and put a match. Then she and Small, carrying their poker and tongs as if afraid of meeting St. Peter, made trips and trips, back and forth, till the Bible table was empty and the ash pile high.

The books had uncanny ways of opening themselves at striking places that made the old ladies squirm. Then a bucket of water made the ash and the hot earth sizzle and warned the flowers "We're coming." Pouf! And a tiny breeze would powder the garden with ash.

The old ladies locked the front door. The grating key said good-bye to the echoes, and the old home was done with Carrs. House and Carrs had given and taken. Good-bye time had come.

1. Flavius Josephus *(37-95?), a Roman-Jewish historian. The book was probably* The Jewish Antiquities *which covers the history of the Jews from the creation of the world. It became popular in an English translation in the 19th century.*

2. Israel Banners: *religious tracts expounding on the mystical significance of heraldry connected with the tribes of Israel, based on certain passages in the Bible.*

MOTHER'S WORK BAG

The bag was not worth a dime, but the Reformed Episcopal Church bazaar charged Mother seventy-five cents for it empty, because it was made by the Bishop's daughter. It was constructed of turkey-red print with a white pin spot and reinforced round its middle by a Chinese cuff-protector of split bamboo. This in turn was decorated by a cut-out Kate Greenaway[1] girl in a puffed skirt. She was of paper, highly coloured and gummed on. There was a drawstring of white tape round the top of the bag. Mother filled it with all the necessary things to keep three little girls, and a boy with the knees always out of his stockings and pants.

The bag hung on the knob at the corner of Mother's bed. Mother had the keenest eye for a missing button. We were buttoned all over: cloth-top button boots, dresses buttoned from the neck to the hem down the back, aprons buttoned all the way down on top of those. Then there were undies buttons and garter buttons and glove buttons. The only thing that was not buttoned

1. Kate Greenaway *(1846-1901) English artist and book illustrator, whose pictures of children clothed in early 19th century garb were enormously popular in the late 19th century.*

onto you was your hat, but that had an elastic that snapped under your chin, and it was always breaking loose from its hat. Then there were our tuckers,[2] a fresh one every day in the neck and sometimes on occasions in the sleeves, too, of our dark-stuff school dresses. They made one look fresh and smart. So Mother's work bag was always busy. I expect it was dearer to me than to the others because I burst more. I was a wide and energetic child.

The old bag is over sixty years old now. I look at it every house-cleaning and every move, when everything seems one too much. But my head shakes and I say: "Not yet, I can't burn it." I am twenty three years older than Mother ever was, yet how I wish that she were here, not to mend my clothes but to mend me.

Please, someone burn Mother's work bag when I am dead. Burn it in the furnace reverently. I could not bear it should be flung in the ash can along with unutterables and go rumbling down the street on Monday, covered with ashes and things that leave a trail of death and smell behind. Please someone put the scarlet pin-spot bag into a private decent home-furnace and watch till it is all burnt, no tags to fly hither and thither.

2. Tucker: *a piece of muslin, lace etc. that is worn around the neck or over the chest.*

DEATH

In the Carr family, we used the word "passed on" or some said, "fell asleep." Small used the good plain word "died" and despised the gentler words.

I have seen six of my immediate family watch approaching death, knowing that he was on the way for them, and that his coming would not be long postponed. I have watched, and wondered, and wondered over again, how did those he was coming for feel about it? Every one in the house knew, yet it might have been the greatest secret. No one mentioned it. They spoke of everything else rather than that. When you were in the sick room, you were supposed to smile and do anything to woo a forgetful merriness out of them for the moment.

You could not look at the sick one and say, "You are dying, how do you feel about it?" My people had been good-living people. It was understood now that good living would stand them in good stead. Did it, I wanted badly to know? Were they frightened, or glad, or sorry, or cross dying? They knew they had to die. Only Father lived out his seventieth year.

The Elder and Bigger attended all the funerals in their church, the Reformed Episcopal, and they loved it when the parson gave deathbed scenes from the pulpit. I though it horrible impertinence of the parson's butting in at the last and not leaving the dying to their own people.

Mother's was the first death in our family. She was a quietly good woman and never preached. She spoke little about death and generally she did not tell us much of what she felt about herself, but gave hints of what we were to do without her to take our troubles to, never of what she was expecting for herself. If we thought of the dreadful lonesomeness of home without her and all started crying, she changed the subject to something else. Mother did not preach. I expect she thought me, a girl of fourteen, too young to talk much to about death. Afterwards I wished I'd asked Mother more; I think she would have been glad to talk if she knew I wanted to.

I was merry and full of life. Middle and Bigger were model children giving no anxiety. After Mother's death when I was unruly, the Elder would say, "You were the one Mother dreaded to leave, being troublesome. For her other children, she had no fear. They did what was expected of them." It hurt cruelly. She knew it and she used it as a lash. I had not realized things would be so difficult without Mother. My sister was a good woman but she had no understanding of children, particularly bad ones.

Father's death was soon after Mother's. He was not ill long. He was seventy and he had always said, "God has set that age as the allotted life of Man." When death came in the late afternoon, we were all about his bed. His eyes roved from one to the other and his hands were restless. It almost seemed as if there was something he wanted to say.

Presently there was a long drawn "Ahah ..." and a footstep on the stair. The Elder rose from her place closest to Father as was proper, being the eldest. She went to the landing. "I am glad you have come, Bishop," she said, and ushered in the Bishop.

Father's hands stopped moving and his eyes stopped roving. The Bishop and Father had been neighbours for many years but they had not been friends, neither had they been enemies. They had a polite formal acquaintance without warmth. The Bishop went to the bedside and took the Elder's place. We young ones were motioned to move further back and retired to the horsehair sofa and dug our red noses into its hard cold shininess while the bishop prayed. He always gasped between each sentence.

There was another dreadful noise in the room which the Bishop's wheeze seemed determined to drown. Presently it stopped and then the Bishop went away. Father was dead.

I said to the Elder, "What was that strange noise the prayer of the Bishop tried to drown?"

"Don't," she said. "His coming was just lucky. I had not sent for him. I had asked Father if he would like a visit from the Bishop and he said, 'No' but the Lord brought him all the same."

"Then I think it was mean. Father never particularly liked him. But that strange noise while the Bishop prayed, what was it?"

"It was the death rattle. The air leaving the lungs."

"Perhaps with that last air Father had wanted to say something to us. Father was shy, he would never speak before the Bishop. It was not fair."

"Hush!" she waggled her long forefinger in my face.

But I went on. "Poor Father, he may have forgotten something or been sorry about something or wanted to explain."

My sister said, "Stop! I did as I thought best. That settles it. Stop I tell you, Miss Settle-everyone's-affairs!"

My brother Dick died away from home. They sent him to California. It was his lungs. During that time there were frequent letters back and forth but death was never mentioned in them, though we knew, and he knew, he could not get better. I was in England when he died.

The Elder's death came as a shock. We had no idea she was so ill, though she had appeared to ail for some while. When the doctor came, he gave her only a few months to live. Bigger came to my house and told me. I was shocked and went down to the old home where the Elder lay. I took her hand and we both choked.

"Now then," she said, "We won't mention it again. I don't want anyone to know." Of course it was that dread disease which everyone likes to hide or calls a "growth." She turned away her face and made some trivial remark.

"How about Nanny, has she been milked this morning?" I said. "Shall I go out and do her?"

"Yes and ring up the goat farm, they wanted to buy her a short while ago," and then she turned her face into the pillow and cried. Cried harder than she had cried about herself. She loved her goat. "Say I want a good home rather than a big price for Nanny."

Next day when they took the goat and I carried the money to her she said, "It's to set my house in order." Nanny was the first step; then she asked to see the lawyer about her will and the parson about her soul.

I was sitting in the room with the nurse when she died. She was unconscious and it was just like the stopping of a clock. The nurse stepped forward and closed her eyes. Death did not seem to be an experience to her. Bigger and Middle went to bed but nurse and I sat by the fire till dawn. Nurse chattered about something. I wanted to be alone.

Bigger died in hospital after a week's illness. After a good night's rest she opened her eyes and died. She had led a very religious life.

You would have expected her to be a saint just in one leap. As to what she thought about her approaching death, she was secret as the grave itself.

I am seventy years old now myself, and for eight years I have been told I may die any minute. I've had strokes and angina. Do I talk about death any more than the others did? No, nor do I wonder about the details of death as I did then. I am content to know that:

Eye hath not seen, neither hath ear heard, the things God has prepared.[1]

And there is a paragraph in **Gitanjali** by Tagore that I think puts death beautifully. Ira gave me the book and more comfort than all the preachers.

I was not aware of the moment when I first crossed
the threshold of this life.
What was the power that made me open out into
this vast mystery like a bud in the forest at midnight?
When in the morning I looked upon the light I felt in a moment
that I was no stranger in this world, that the inscrutable without name
and form had taken me in its arms in the form of my own mother.
Even so, in death, the same unknown will appear as ever known to me.
And because I love this life, I know I shall love death as well.
The child cries out when from the right breast the mother takes it
away, in the very next moment to find in the left one its consolation.[2]

---

1. *Emily is referring to: I Corinthians 2:9, a passage from the King James version of the* Bible. *It reads: "But as it is written, Eye hath not seen, nor ear heard, neither have entered into the heart of man, the things which God hath prepared for them that love him."*

2. *From section 95 of* Gitanjali *by Rabindranath Tagore.*

RED ROSES

I was in a nursing home sick. Someone sent me a bunch of red rose buds, hard and tight and round. They unfurled to maturity slowly in the cool of my room. At last they showed their golden hearts, and as soon as they had done so, a subtle change came over them. Their secret was out and their scarlet turned to red-purple. Matron said, "Away with them to the garbage can!" But I pled, there is beauty in them yet, and flowers are so scarce now.

It was evening, the hour when warm dinnery smells pervaded the halls and whiffs of other people's trays came a-visiting. I had finished my meal and lay in the drowsy dark. My arm restlessly flung itself across the table beside my bed. I felt the coolness of the roses against my hand, and separating one from his fellows, I laid it over one hot burning eye. I had been crying. Just a little. It was very soothing and I took another rose and laid it over my other eyelid. Then I went to sleep quieted.

An hour later, I awoke to the clank and clatter of dishes being washed below. I put my hand up and snatched the roses off my eyes. The nurse would think I was crazy. I returned them to the vase, the near side, a little apart from their fellows.

Nurse bustled in with a crunch of starched garments and clipped the lights on. I looked at the roses; the two near me—the two that had lain across my eyes—had returned to their original scarlet. The blue-red bloom of withering had left them. They had not renewed their youngness, just their colour.

I kept them another week and the scarlet red never went back to the bruised purple oldness. The two eyelid roses remained scarletty. Their leaves crisped and petals dropped but they were red till Matron took them out one night and they never came back.

I do not know the reason, but my eyes and my roses knew it was so, that my eyes gave those roses back their scarlet.

HOARDING FOR OLD AGE

Have I squirrel blood in me? Some of their characteristics are in me very strong. One is my keen appetite for nuts, but my strongest squirrel way (and I've had it as far back as I can remember) is hoarding. Not money or things that you can touch with your hands, but hoarding experience.

When I was a child, I was very fond of old ladies. There were several I used to read to and a lot that I went to visit, old ladies who sat in chairs all day. I wondered what they thought about, sitting with their wrinkled hands folded in their laps. "I hope they have lots of nice thoughts stored up in their heads," I used to say to myself.

For loneliness the married did not seem much better off than the unmarried. Maybe they did have children and grandchildren, but the children seemed too busy minding the grandchildren and grandchildren seemed very bored with Grand's long stories and long kissings. Having more people to love only gave one more people to trouble over.

Well, I looked at all these old people and I said: "Emily, see all you can with your young eyes, hear all you can with your young ears, because if you don't have your memory full, old age is going to be very dull!" I went everywhere I got the chance to go, and I saw and heard and hoarded. Though I really had no idea how much these hoardings were going to help my old age, nor how much they now enriched my life during the years I was hoarding for my oldness.

When I heard grownups discussing a place that interested me, I would tell myself: "Emily you must go to that place, you will get lots of rememberings to hoard there," and nearly always I went sooner or later. Sometimes it took scrimping and pinching in other ways, but I went somehow.

The first trip I remember definitely planning in this way came about through hearing a nurse who came to see my mother. She and my mother were chatting, I listening. She had been up among the mountains of Yale, B.C. She was not an educated woman but she must have been a vivid narrator. She said, "Yale is very hot in summer. You see, Yale sits in a little basin."

The phrase caught my fancy: surrounded by high mountains all round, sitting in a basin like a baby in its bath. I sat listening quietly, not joining into the talk or asking questions. I just saw Yale sitting in a bath of heat. "Someday I must see this little town, sitting in a basin."

I did, but not till I was an adult and took myself there to sketch. It was midwinter, white and frozen, otherwise everything was just as that nurse had said. I was in a cold hotel. Strangely, I never felt Yale cold, always hot. The rememberings of that old nurse had been vivid, more vivid than the findings of my own adult eyes.

A French artist and his English artist wife came to Victoria. She painted better than he did and he was jealous. They were the first real artists I had ever known. I believed everything they said. They told me how marvellous was London and to see Paris! Why, they were the only places in the world to paint in. You did not even have to study much in Paris to learn painting, all you did was to go there and look and absorb things and talk to artists, and there you were—a painter!

"Emily," I told myself, "You certainly must go to London and to Paris, no matter what the cost," and eventually I went. It was not as easy as they said, it meant work—hard work– to get there and to become. If I had not gone I would never really have been happy over my work for hankering.

It was the way all my life. If I wanted things hard enough, and I strove and I managed, somehow they came my way. Sometimes it was just an Indian village I heard of, off the beaten track and hard to get àt. Sometimes it was a person or a doing, but somehow or other they came my way, but always I had to do my share and go out to meet them.

These things were like Father's jar of Hundreds and Thousands candies, so small that alone you couldn't even call each a candy. Father said, "Hold out your hands!" and he poured Hundreds and Thousands into our palms. We bobbed our heads down, and our tongues out, and there we were—a pretty taste, sweet and crunchy, made by those tiny bits of things that were nothings in themselves.

THE END

Alphabetical List Of Stories

CHRONOLOGY OF EMILY CARR

1871 — Born December 13, Victoria, British Columbia.

1879 — (Emily 7) Begins to attend Mrs. Fraser's Private
School. Takes art lessons from Miss Emily Woods.

1886 — (Emily 14) Death of Emily's mother.

1888 — Death of Emily's father.

1889 — Completes her last year of High School.

1890 — (Emily 18) Studies art in San Francisco.

1893 — Returns to Victoria.

Teaches children's art classes in the "Barn Studio"

1894 — Wins prize for drawing at Victoria Agricultural Fair.

1899 — (Emily 27) First trip to Ucluelet to sketch in early spring.

Leaves Victoria to study art in England.

1901 — Visit from Alice. Emily studying in the countryside.

1902 — (Emily 30) Emily suffers breakdown.

1903 —Lizzie comes and takes her to Sanatorium in East Anglia.

1904 — Returns to Victoria. Visits Toronto and Cariboo on the way.
Second visit to Ucluelet.

1905 — Cartoonist for *The Week*. Teaching in Victoria.

Has an art studio on Fort Street.

1906 — (Emily 34) Moves to Vancouver. Teaching art to
children. Meets Sophie Frank.

1907 — Visit to Alaska, stops at Alert Bay. Decides to visit
Indian sites and paint a record of their vanishing villages.

1908-1909 — Summer trips to: Alert Bay, Campbell River,
Cape Mudge on Quadra Island, Sechelt and up the
Fraser River to Hope, Yale and Lytton.

1910 — Exhibition at Granville Street studio. Moves to France. (Alice goes with her but does not stay)

1911 — Takes a short trip to Sweden. Returns to Vancouver. Rents studio at 1465 West Broadway.

1912 — (Emily 40) Six-week trip to Indian villages.

1913 — Big show in Drummond Hall. Returns to Victoria. Builds Hill House (House of All Sorts).

1916 — (Emily 45) Works in San Francisco doing painting and wall decorations for the St. Francis Hotel ballroom.

1917 — Sets up kennels to raise bobtail dogs for sale.

1918 — Cartoonist for *Western Women's Weekly*.

1919 — Deaths of two older sisters, Clara and Edith.

1920 — (Emily 50) Emily resumes annual summer travels.

1924 — Exhibits in Seattle. Meets Mark Tobey. Starts to produce pottery.

1926 — Starts a short story writing course by correspondence.

1927 — (Emily 55) Travels to eastern Canada and meets Group of Seven. Participates in "Canadian West Coast Art: Native and Modern" at the National Gallery of Canada in Ottawa.

1928 — Travels to Queen Charlotte Islands, and up the Skeena and Nass rivers. Exhibits summer's work at 646 Simcoe St.

1930 — Second trip to eastern Canada. Shows work with Group of Seven. Visits New York City to view modern art.

1932 — "People's Gallery" opened in December, lasts only a few months.

1933 — (Emily 61) Sketching trip to British Columbia Interior. Purchase of the "Elephant" (camper-trailer). Final trip East.

1934 — Summer school course in short story writing in Victoria.

1936 — Sale of Hill House, move to Beckley Street.

Death of Lizzie. Makes her last trip in the Elephant.

A public viewing of work in her cottage at 316 Beckley St.

1937 — First heart attack. Successful solo exhibition at Art Gallery of Ontario.

1938 — Very successful solo exhibition at Vancouver Art Gallery.

1939 — Emily's second heart attack. Camps for three weeks in Langford.

1940 — Move from Beckley Street to share Alice's house.

Major stroke. Broadcast of *Klee Wyck* stories on CBC Radio.

1941 — (Emily 69) Publication of *Klee Wyck*. The book goes on to receive a Governor General's Award for Literature.

1942 — Last sketching trip. Major heart attack.

Publication of *The Book of Small*.

1943 — Solo exhibitions in Montreal, Toronto, Vancouver, Seattle.

Emily is hospitalized with another stroke. Begins to write her "Hundreds and Thousands" stories.

1944 — (Emily 72) Still paints in Beacon Hill from wheelchair.

Publication of *The House of All Sorts*. Third stroke.

1945 — Enters St. Mary's Priory (now the James Bay Inn).

Emily's last heart attack. Dies March 2 at age 73.

1946 — Publication of *Growing Pains*.

1953 — Publication of two books: *Pause: A Sketch Book* and *The Heart of a Peacock*.

1966 — Publication of *Hundreds and Thousands*: (The Journals).

2006 — Publication of *Wild Flowers*.

2007 — Publication of *This and That*.